# American Headway

Workbook **1**

### THE WORLD'S MOST TRUSTED ENGLISH COURSE

SECOND EDITION

**Liz and John Soars**
**Sylvia Wheeldon**

Spotlight on Testing lessons
by Lawrence J. Zwier

OXFORD
UNIVERSITY PRESS

# Contents

You will need to listen to the Student Workbook CD for some exercises. If you do not have the Student Workbook CD, you can access the audio files on the *American Headway* Student Audio Download Center or read the Audio Scripts on pages 68–69.

# 1 Hello everybody!

**Grammar:** *am/is/are* • *my/your/ his/her* • *a or an?*
**Vocabulary:** Countries and nationalities • Letters and numbers 1–20

## *am/is/are*

### 1 What's your name?

**CD** **2** Complete the conversations.

1. **A** Hello. What's your name?

   **B** Emma. What's _____ _____ ?

   **A** My name _____ Lisa. Where _____ you _____, Emma?

   **B** I _____ from Toronto. _____ _____ you from?

   2. **A** _____ _____ Boston.

   2. **C** Hello. _____ _____ Miguel. _____ a student.

## 2 I'm from Mexico

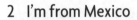

Write sentences.

1. Miguel

   **I'm from Mexico.**

2. Lisa and Mike

   **We're from the U.S.**

3. Akiko and Miho

   _____

4. So-young

   _____

5. Pietro and Franco

   _____

6. Rosa

   _____

7. Kai

   _____

8. Jason

   _____

## 3 She's a teacher from Russia

Write about the people.

| | |
|---|---|
| Last name | Mariskova |
| First name | Svetlana |
| From | Russia |
| Job | Teacher |
| Age | 30 |

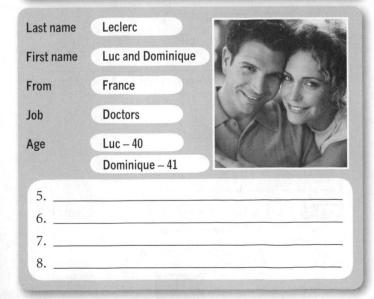

*She's Svetlana Mariskova.*
*She's from Russia.*
*She's a teacher.*
*She's 30.*

| | |
|---|---|
| Last name | Costa |
| First name | Tiago |
| From | Brazil |
| Job | Student |
| Age | 19 |

1. _____
2. _____
3. _____
4. _____

| | |
|---|---|
| Last name | Leclerc |
| First name | Luc and Dominique |
| From | France |
| Job | Doctors |
| Age | Luc – 40 |
| | Dominique – 41 |

5. _____
6. _____
7. _____
8. _____

## 4 Long forms

Write the long forms.

1. I'm a student.
   **I am a student.**

2. What's your name?
   _____

3. He's from Japan.
   _____

4. I'm 15 years old.
   _____

5. They're from the United States.
   _____

6. You're American.
   _____

7. We're students.

## 5 Short forms

Write the short forms.

1. She is a student.
   **She's a student.**

2. My name is Rosa.
   _____

3. She is married.
   _____

4. They are from Taiwan.
   _____

5. I am from Chile. I am not from Argentina.
   _____

6. We are from the United States.
   _____

7. He is a teacher. He is not a doctor.
   _____

# Possessive adjectives

## 6 *my* and *your*

Complete the sentences with *my* or *your*.

1. Hello. _____ name's Emma.
2. What's _____ name?
3. Is Jenny _____ sister?

4. **Miguel** Emma, this is _____ friend, Carlos.
   **Emma** Hello, Carlos. And this is _____
   sister, Jenny.
   **Carlos** Hi, Jenny.

## 7 *his* and *her*

Complete the sentences with *his* or *her*.

1. **A** What's _____ name?
   **B** Lisa.
2. _____ name is Mike Brown.
3. I have a brother. _____ name is Hiro.
4. Rosa is from Spain. _____ apartment is
   in Barcelona.

4   Unit 1 · Hello everybody!

# Vocabulary and pronunciation

## 8 Countries and nationalities

**CD 3** Match the countries and nationalities.

| Country | Nationality |
|---------|-------------|
| England | Australian |
| Canada | Spanish |
| Italy | Korean |
| France | English |
| Spain | Japanese |
| China | Canadian |
| Australia | Brazilian |
| Japan | Russian |
| the U.S. | Italian |
| Mexico | French |
| Russia | American |
| Korea | Chinese |
| Brazil | Mexican |

## 9 Where's the stress?

1. **CD 4** Put these two-syllable words into the
   correct column.

   | ~~England~~ | ~~Japan~~ | Russia | Russian |
   |---------|---------|--------|---------|
   | Brazil | Spanish | China | English |

   | •• | •• |
   |---------|---------|
   | England | Japan |
   | _____ | _____ |
   | _____ | _____ |
   | _____ | _____ |
   | _____ | |

2. **CD 5** Put these three-syllable words into the
   correct column.

   | ~~Canada~~ Mexico ~~Korean~~ Italy Australian |
   |---|

   | •• | •• |
   |---------|---------|
   | Canada | Korean |
   | _____ | _____ |
   | _____ | |

3. **CD 6** Look at these four-syllable words. They all have
   the same stress. Is it •••• or ••••?

   | Canadian   American   Brazilian |
   |---|

# a or an?

## 10 What's this in English?

Write *a*, *an*, or the plural noun.

1. **a bag**

 2. **an ice cream**

 3. **keys**

4. _____

5. _____

6. _____

7. _____

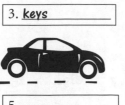

8. _____

9. _____

10. _____

11. _____

12. _____

## 11 An American car

Complete the sentences with words from the boxes.

|     |               |            |
| --- | ------------- | ---------- |
|     | American      | car        |
|     | French        | university |
|     | international | city       |
| a   | English       | camera     |
| an  | Japanese      | drink      |
|     | Korean        | language   |
|     | Italian       | car        |

1. A Cadillac is **an American car**.
2. A cappuccino is _____.
3. A Nikon is _____.
4. English is _____.
5. Paris is _____.
6. A Hyundai is _____.
7. Oxford is _____.

# Check it

## 12 Right or wrong?

Put a check (✔) next to the correct sentence.

1. ☐ His from Korea.
   ✔ He's from Korea.

2. ✔ She's a teacher.
   ☐ She's teacher.

3. ☐ Where she from?
   ☐ Where's she from?

4. ☐ What's her name?
   ☐ What's she name?

5. ☐ I'm a student.
   ☐ I'm student.

6. ☐ I have two sisters.
   ☐ I have two sister.

7. ☐ They from Japan.
   ☐ They're from Japan.

8. ☐ It's a Spanish orange.
   ☐ It's an Spanish orange.

9. ☐ He's name's Miguel.
   ☐ His name's Miguel.

10. ☐ Her name is Emma.
    ☐ Her name it's Emma.

## 13 Translation

Translate the sentences.

1. What's your name?

_____

2. I'm Miguel.

_____

3. He's a doctor.

_____

4. They're from the U.S.

_____

5. She's 18.

_____

6. How are you?

_____

7. I'm fine, thanks. And you?

_____

8. Good-bye. See you later!

_____

## 14 Listening – Hello and good-bye

**CD 7** Listen. Put the conversation in the correct order.

| 1 | Hello, Lisa! How are you? |
|---|---|
| ☐ | Fine, thanks! See you at 7:00 in the cafe? |
| ☐ | OK, thanks, Mike. And you? |
| ☐ | Thanks, you too. Bye, Lisa! |
| ☐ | Bye, Mike. |
| ☐ | Yes, see you later, Mike. Have a nice day! |

# Letters and numbers

## 15 The alphabet

**CD 8** Match the letters with the same vowel sound.

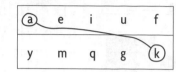

| a | e | i | u | f |
|---|---|---|---|---|
| y | m | q | g | k |

| c | h | s | w |
|---|---|---|---|
| j | u | f | v |

## 16 1–20

Match the numbers and words.

| | | | | | | | | | |
|---|---|---|---|---|---|---|---|---|---|
| 10 | seven | 2 | nine | 7 | eight | 15 | three | 17 |
| twelve | 18 | fourteen | 5 | two | 20 | seventeen |
| 4 | ten | 9 | five | 13 | four | 11 | nineteen | fifteen |
| 12 | eleven | 8 | eighteen | 14 | twenty | 16 | one |
| 3 | sixteen | 6 | thirteen | 19 | six | 1 |

## 17 How many?

Write the numbers and objects.

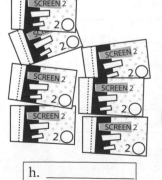

a. _two apples_

b. _____

c. _____

d. _____

e. _____

f. _____

g. _____

h. _____

i. _____

j. _____

**Grammar:** Questions and negatives •
Possessive 's
**Vocabulary:** Adjectives and nouns •
Plural nouns • Numbers 1–100 and
prices

## Questions and negatives

### 1 Question words

Match the questions and answers.

| | |
|---|---|
| 1. Where's the Empire State Building? | a. (212) 347-3213. |
| 2. How are you? | b. Twenty-one. |
| 3. How old are you? | c. Tom Smith. |
| 4. What's your phone number? | d. It's in New York. |
| 5. Who's your teacher? | e. Fine, thanks. |

### 2 Making questions

1 **CD 9** Read about the Mariskova family.

# THE MARISKOVA family

Svetlana is a Russian teacher. She's thirty.
She's at school now. Her address is 18 Sretenka
Street, Moscow.

Her husband, Mikhail, is at work in his office.
He's a bank manager. His phone number at work
is 095 097 7321.

They have two children, Maria and Alina. Maria
is ten and Alina is seven. They are at school.

2  Write questions for these answers.

**About the family**

1. Where <u>are they from</u>  ?       Moscow, Russia.

**About Svetlana**

2. What's <u>her job</u>      ?       She's a teacher.
3. How _____ ?       She's thirty.
4. Where _____ now ?   At school.
5. What's _____ ?       18 Sretenka Street,
                             Moscow.

**About Mikhail**

6. Where _____ ?       In his office.
7. _____ ?       He's a bank manager.
8. _____ ?       095 097 7321.

**About the children**

9. _____ ?       Ten and seven.
10. _____ ?       At school.

## 3 Listening – Asking questions

**CD 10** Listen to the questions and answers. Complete the information.

Last name ..........................
First name Diana ..................
Country ............................
Address .......... Charles Street,
Apartment ...... , New York
..................................
Phone number ....................
Job ...............................
Age ..............................
Married    Yes/No

## 4 Questions about you

**CD 11** Answer the questions about you.

1. What's your last name? _____
2. What's your first name? _____
3. Where are you from? _____
4. What's your job? _____
5. What's your address? _____
6. What's your phone number? _____
7. How old are you? _____
8. Are you married? _____

## 5 Making negatives

Correct the sentences.

1. Brazil is in Europe.
   **Brazil isn't in Europe. It's in South America.**

2. The president of the United States is English.
   _____

3. Moscow is in Germany.
   _____

4. Five and six is twelve.
   _____

5. You're English.
   _____

6. We're in a Russian class.
   _____

7. Rolls-Royce cars are cheap.
   _____

## 6 Short answers

**CD 12** Write true answers.

1. Are you English?          No, I'm not.
2. Are you a student?        Yes, I am.
3. Is your teacher married?  _____
4. Is it Monday today?       _____
5. Is English difficult?     _____
6. Are you twenty-one years old? _____
7. Are you at school?        _____
8. Are your parents at home? _____

## 7 Short forms

Write the short forms.

1. Italy is in Europe.        Italy's in Europe.
2. It is not Monday today.    _____
3. I am not married.          _____
4. Where is the newspaper?    _____
5. They are not from Boston.  _____
6. We are at work.            _____
7. You are a student.         _____
8. I am fine, thanks.         _____

## 8 Long forms

Write the long forms.

1. They're Italian.           They are Italian.
2. You aren't in New York.    _____
3. My apartment's small.      _____
4. Her son isn't an actor.    _____
5. His wife's a journalist.   _____
6. They're at work.           _____
7. We aren't old.             _____
8. We're OK, thanks.          _____

# Vocabulary 1

## 9 Listening – A family tree

**CD 13** Look at the family tree. Listen and write the names in the correct places.

| Mary | Shannon | Laura | Connor |

~ THE BINCHEY FAMILY ~

David = _____

Patrick = Bonnie _____ = Ethan

_____ Brian Heather _____

Look at the family tree and complete the sentences.

1. Bonnie **is Patrick's** wife.
2. Brian _____ _____ brother.
3. Connor _____ Ethan and Shannon's _____ .
4. Bonnie _____ Connor and Heather's _____ .
5. Ethan _____ _____ husband.
6. Mary _____ Laura, Brian, Connor, and Heather's _____ .
7. Patrick _____ Connor and Heather's _____ .
8. Shannon _____ Patrick's _____ .

## 10 Your family

Draw your family tree. Write about your family.

# Possessive 's

## 11 It's Sara's bag

Look at the pictures. Write sentences.

1. _It's Sara's bag._

2. _____

3. _____

4. _____

5. _____

6. _____

## 12 Possessive 's or is?

Write **P** if 's = possession.
Write **is** if 's = is.

1. John's car is new. **P**
2. It's a Mercedes. **is**
3. It's Tuesday today. _____
4. David's a doctor. _____
5. David's wife is fifty-five. _____
6. His father's in Ireland. _____
7. My son's apartment is very nice. _____
8. My daughter's school is good. _____
9. Erin's a teacher. _____
10. Erin's school is in the center of the city. _____

# Vocabulary 2

## 13 Adjectives and nouns

Look at the pictures. Describe them using the words from the box.

| | | |
|---|---|---|
| | exciting | man |
| | expensive | exercise |
| | fast | day |
| a | easy | city |
| an | hot | car |
| | difficult | girl |
| | old | camera |
| | young | language |

1. *an exciting city*
2. _____
3. _____
4. _____
5. _____
6. _____
7. _____
8. _____

# Plural nouns

## 14 Spelling of plural nouns

Write the plural forms of the nouns.

1. car _____
2. class _____
3. city _____
4. woman _____
5. family _____
6. address _____
7. person _____
8. day _____
9. sandwich _____
10. university _____

# Check it

## 15 Translation

Translate the sentences.

1. How old are you?
   _____

2. What's her job?
   _____

3. Are you married? No, I'm not.
   _____
   _____

4. She isn't a doctor.
   _____

5. What's your mother's name?
   _____

6. Good morning. Can I help?
   _____
   _____

7. Can I have a coffee, please?
   _____

8. Here you are. Anything else?
   _____
   _____

# Numbers and prices

## 16 1–100

**1** **CD 14** Study the numbers.

| | | | | | | | |
|---|---|---|---|---|---|---|---|
| 1 | one | 11 | eleven | 21 | twenty-one | 31 | thirty-one |
| 2 | two | 12 | twelve | 22 | twenty-two | 40 | forty |
| 3 | three | 13 | thirteen | 23 | twenty-three | 50 | fifty |
| 4 | four | 14 | fourteen | 24 | twenty-four | 60 | sixty |
| 5 | five | 15 | fifteen | 25 | twenty-five | 70 | seventy |
| 6 | six | 16 | sixteen | 26 | twenty-six | 80 | eighty |
| 7 | seven | 17 | seventeen | 27 | twenty-seven | 90 | ninety |
| 8 | eight | 18 | eighteen | 28 | twenty-eight | 100 | one hundred |
| 9 | nine | 19 | nineteen | 29 | twenty-nine | | |
| 10 | ten | 20 | twenty | 30 | thirty | | |

**2** Write the numbers. Read them aloud.

| | | | |
|---|---|---|---|
| one | _1_ | two | _____ |
| ten | _____ | twelve | _____ |
| one hundred | _____ | twenty | _____ |
| 3 | _____ | fourteen | _____ |
| 13 | _____ | forty-five | _____ |
| 30 | _____ | fifty-four | _____ |
| 5 | _____ | sixteen | _____ |
| 15 | _____ | twenty-six | _____ |
| 50 | _____ | sixty-one | _____ |
| 7 | _____ | eighteen | _____ |
| 17 | _____ | eighty-seven | _____ |
| 78 | _____ | ninety-eight | _____ |
| 19 | _____ | 40 | _____ |
| 90 | _____ | 65 | _____ |
| 99 | _____ | 82 | _____ |

## 17 How much?

Do the calculations. Write the answer in two ways.

1. How much is 60¢ and 55¢?

   <u>**$1.15.**</u>

   <u>**One dollar and fifteen cents.**</u>

2. How much is 20¢ and 70¢?

   _____

   _____

3. How much is 90¢ and 40¢?

   _____

   _____

4. How much is $6.80 and 35¢?

   _____

   _____

5. How much is $9.50 and $4.25?

   _____

   _____

6. How much is $33 and $48?

   _____

   _____

7. How much is $50 and $75.50?

   _____

   _____

# 3

# The world of work

**Grammar:** Present Simple 1 •
Questions and negatives
**Vocabulary:** Jobs • Daily routines •
Verbs and nouns • Time

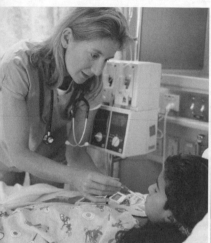

**She's a nurse.**

_She wears a uniform._
_____
_____
_____

**He's a journalist.**

_____
_____
_____
_____

**He's a sales assistant.**

_____
_____
_____
_____

**She's an interpreter.**

_____
_____
_____
_____

## Present Simple 1

### 1 What does he/she do?

Write the sentences in the correct columns on the left.

~~She wears a uniform.~~
She works in a hospital.
He helps people.
He sells things.
She helps sick people.
She works at the United Nations.
He works in a newspaper office.
He takes money.
She meets people from different countries.
She speaks three languages.
He works on a computer.
He works in a store.
He asks people questions.
She translates things.
He writes a lot.
She works with doctors.

### 2 Spelling of the third person singular

Complete the sentences with a verb from the box.

| start   have   go   study   live   fly   play   ~~speak~~ |

1. He **_speaks_** four languages.

2. Julia _____ in an apartment in Miami.

3. She's a pilot. She _____ all over the world.

4. Peter _____ two children.

5. In the winter Alice _____ skiing and in the
   summer she _____ tennis.

6. My daughter _____ Japanese at school.

7. John _____ work at six o'clock every day.

## 3  Daily routines

1  What do you do first in the day? What do you do next? Number the activities in the correct order for you.

| | |
|---|---|
| ☐ have lunch | ☐ have dinner |
| ☐ take a shower | ☐ watch television |
| ☐ go to work | ☐ 1 get up |
| ☐ have breakfast | ☐ read a book |
| ☐ start work | ☐ go to bed |
| ☐ go home | ☐ leave home |
| ☐ get dressed | |

2  **CD 15**  Complete the sentences about Rupert's day. Use the correct form of the verbs in Exercise 1.

1. Rupert **gets up** _____ at seven o'clock.
2. He _____ .
3. Then he _____ .
4. He _____ coffee and toast for breakfast.
5. He _____ his apartment at eight-thirty.
6. He _____ to work by bus.
7. He works in a bookstore. He _____ work at nine o'clock.
8. At one o'clock he _____ lunch in a small cafe.
9. He leaves work at five-thirty and _____ home.
10. First he _____ dinner.
11. Then he _____ television.
12. He _____ to bed at eleven o'clock and _____ a book.

# Questions and negatives

## 4  Questions about Rupert

1  Make the questions for the answers about Rupert in Exercise 2.

1. does / what / up / get / he / time / ?
   **What time does he get up?**

2. for / does / have / breakfast / he / what / ?
   _____

3. to / how / he / work / does / get / ?
   _____

4. lunch / where / have / does / he / ?
   _____

5. he / does / what / evenings / do / the / in / ?
   _____

6. bed / does / to / when / he / go / ?
   _____

2  Write the questions for these answers.

1. _____ ?  At nine o'clock.
2. _____ ?  In a bookstore.
3. _____ ?  At one o'clock.
4. _____ ?  At five-thirty.
5. _____ doing in the evenings?  He likes watching TV and reading.

Rupert's Day

## 5 Question words

Match the questions and answers.

| | |
|---|---|
| 1. Where does he live? | a. Thirty-two. |
| 2. What does she do in her free time? | b. Because he's a pilot. |
| 3. Who does he play basketball with? | c. In an apartment in Chicago. |
| 4. When does she play tennis? | d. His two sons. |
| 5. How does he get to work? | e. By car. |
| 6. How many languages does she speak? | f. Two. Spanish and English. |
| 7. How old are you? | g. She goes swimming. |
| 8. Why does he travel a lot? | h. In the summer. |

## 6 *does*, *is*, or *has*?

Complete the conversation with *does*, *is*, or *has*.

A My sister ＿＿＿＿＿ very beautiful.

B What ＿＿＿＿＿ she do?

A She ＿＿＿＿＿ a model.

B Where ＿＿＿＿＿ she live?

A She ＿＿＿＿＿ a nice apartment in Paris.

B ＿＿＿＿＿ she speak French?

A Yes, she ＿＿＿＿＿.

B ＿＿＿＿＿ she married?

A Yes. Her husband's name ＿＿＿＿＿ Marcel.

B ＿＿＿＿＿ she have any children?

A Yes. She ＿＿＿＿＿ one son. He ＿＿＿＿＿ three years old.

## 7 Listening – Asking for information

**CD 16** Listen. Complete the information about Hiroshi Fukuda.

**HIROSHI FUKUDA**

| | |
|---|---|
| **Name** | Hiroshi Fukuda |
| **Country** | ＿＿＿＿＿＿＿＿＿＿＿＿＿ |
| **Job** | ＿＿＿＿＿＿＿＿＿＿＿＿＿ |
| **City** | ＿＿＿＿＿＿＿＿＿＿＿＿＿ |
| **Place of work** | at ＿＿＿＿＿, and he travels a lot |
| **Languages** | ＿＿＿＿＿ , ＿＿＿＿＿ , and Korean |
| **Family** | married to Nina, ＿＿＿＿＿＿＿＿＿＿＿＿＿＿＿＿＿ |
| **Free time** | ＿＿＿＿＿＿＿＿＿＿＿＿＿ |

## 8 Yes/No questions

1 **CD 17** Look at the questionnaire about Kurt and Gloria. Listen and check the boxes.

| Does he/she ... ? | KURT | GLORIA |
|---|---|---|
| live in a city | ☐ | ☐ |
| speak a foreign language | ☐ | ☐ |
| have a dog | ☐ | ☐ |
| like listening to music | ☐ | ☐ |
| like his/her job | ☐ | ☐ |

2 Write short answers about Kurt.

1. Does Kurt live in a city? **Yes, he does.**
2. Does he speak a foreign language? _____
3. Does he have a dog? _____
4. Does he like listening to music? _____
5. Does he like his job? _____. He's a pilot.

3 Here are the answers to some Yes/No questions about Gloria. Write the questions.

1. **Does she live in a city?** _____
   No, she doesn't. She lives in a small town.
2. _____
   Yes, she does. She speaks English, Portuguese, and Spanish.
3. _____
   No, she doesn't. But she has a cat.
4. _____
   Yes, she does.
5. _____
   Yes, she does. She's a tour guide.

## 9 Making negatives

1 Complete the sentences about Gloria and Kurt.

1. Gloria **doesn't live** _____ in a city.
2. She _____ a dog.
3. Kurt _____ three foreign languages.
4. He _____ listening to music.
5. He _____ a dog.

2 Correct the sentences.

1. A journalist sells things.
   **A journalist doesn't sell things. A journalist writes for a newspaper.**
2. The President lives in New York.
   _____
3. Our teacher arrives late every day.
   _____
4. An architect translates things.
   _____
5. School starts at six o'clock in the morning.
   _____
6. *American Headway* teaches German.
   _____

# Check it

## 10 Translation

Translate these sentences.

1. He comes from Budapest in Hungary.
   _____
2. What does she do?
   _____
3. Pamela's a doctor.
   _____
4. He's married to Nina.
   _____
5. A nurse takes care of people in a hospital.
   _____
6. Excuse me. Can you tell me the time, please?
   _____
7. Yes, of course.
   _____
8. It's about three o'clock.
   _____

# Vocabulary revision

## 11 Verbs and nouns

Match a verb in **A** with a noun or phrase in **B**.

| A | B |
|---|---|
| 1. take | a. a car |
| 2. watch | b. the phone |
| 3. read | c. tennis |
| 4. go | d. television |
| 5. play | e. in an apartment |
| 6. drive | f. a shower |
| 7. wear | g. a magazine |
| 8. live | h. a uniform |
| 9. answer | i. by bus |

## 12 Word groups

Put the words into the correct list.

| | | | | |
|---|---|---|---|---|
| house | boat | hospital | lawyer | taxi |
| bus | country | interpreter | busy | nurse |
| city | pilot | exciting | new | actor |
| car | awful | office | plane | cheap |

**Jobs**

_____

_____

_____

_____

_____

**Places**

_____

_____

_____

_____

_____

**Transportation**

_____

_____

_____

_____

**Adjectives**

_____

_____

_____

_____

## 13 What time is it?

1 Write the times. Practice saying them.

1. _It's three-thirty._     7. _____

2. _____     8. _____

3. _____     9. _____

4. _____     10. _____

5. _____     11. _____

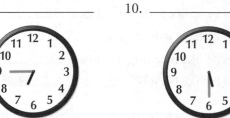

6. _____     12. _____

2 **CD 18** Listen and write the times. Write the numbers.

1. _____ **4:15** _____     4. _____

2. _____     5. _____

3. _____     6. _____

# 4 Take it easy!

## Present Simple 2

### 1 She lives in Mexico and works in California

1 Read about Kate Adams. Complete the sentences with the correct verb from the box.

| | | | |
|---|---|---|---|
| costs | comes | lives | doesn't work |
| doesn't want | loves | is | works | travels |

## "My weekends fly by!"

Kate Adams (1) _____ 48 and (2) _____ from the West Coast of the United States. She (3) _____ in Mexico City because her husband's job is there. Kate (4) _____ in a grocery store on weekends, but she (5) _____ in Mexico. She (6) _____ 3,034 km to work every week—in California! The trip (7) _____ $400, but she (8) _____ her job and (9) _____ to stop.

2 Complete the text with the correct form of the verb.

"I (1) _____ (leave) home every Thursday afternoon, and my husband usually (2) _____ (drive) me to the Mexico City airport in the car. The people at the airport (3) _____ (know) me now and they (4) _____ (say) hello when I (5) _____ (walk) in. Then I (6) _____ (fly) to the San Francisco airport and (7) _____ (take) a taxi to my hometown, Sausalito. I (8) _____ (stay) with my mom and dad. I (9) _____ (work) at the grocery store on Friday and Saturday afternoons and all day on Sundays. I (10) _____ (love) my job and I (11) _____ (not arrive) late! My evenings are busy. My friends (12) _____ (visit) me, and we always (13) _____ (go out) on Saturday nights. I (14) _____ (have) a lot of good friends in Sausalito—they (15) _____ (think) I'm a bit crazy! On Sunday evenings I (16) _____ (go back) to Mexico and my husband sometimes (17) _____ (meet) me at the airport. I (18) _____ (not get up) early on Monday morning! My husband (19) _____ (not work) on Mondays, because he (20) _____ (work) all weekend. So we usually (21) _____ (have) a nice day together!"

3 Ask Kate questions.

1. What **do** you **do** ?
   I work in a grocery store.
2. What _____ your husband _____?
   He's a hotel manager.
3. Where _____ you _____?
   In Mexico City.
4. How many languages _____ you _____?
   Only English.
5. _____ you _____ Spanish?
   Only a little. But I want to learn it.
6. _____ your husband _____ Spanish?
   Yes, he does. He speaks it fluently.
7. Where _____ you _____?
   In a grocery store in Sausalito, California!
8. Why _____ you _____ working there?
   Because I love my job, and I see my friends and family every week.

## 2 We want to go on vacation

**CD 19** Mr. and Mrs. Smith are with a travel agent. Listen and put the conversation in the correct order.

**Travel agent**

a. ☐ Sure. Where do you want to go?

b. ☐ Children? How many children do you have?

c. ☐ 1 Good morning. Can I help you?

d. ☐ French! That gives me a good idea! I think I have the perfect winter vacation for your family!

e. ☐ And how old are they? What do they like doing?

**Mr. and Mrs. Smith**

f. ☐ Yes, please. My husband and I want to go on a winter vacation.

g. ☐ Well. Our son's twelve. He loves all sports—skiing, swimming, football ... Our daughter is sixteen. She doesn't like sports. She likes sunbathing, reading, drinking coffee ... And she wants to practice her French.

h. ☐ Two ... two children, a son and a daughter.

i. ☐ Well. This is the problem. I like skiing and winter sports, but my husband doesn't. He wants to relax and sit in the sun, and the children ...

## 3 Short answers

1 Write short answers to the questions about the Smith family. Use *do*, *does*, *don't*, and *doesn't*.

1. Do they want a summer vacation?      No, they <u>don't</u> .

2. Do they want a winter vacation?      Yes, they _____ .

3. Do Mr. Smith and his daughter like skiing?      No, they _____ .

4. Do Mrs. Smith and her son like skiing?      Yes, they _____ .

5. Does their daughter like sports?      No, she _____ .

6. Does their daughter speak French?      Yes, she _____ .

2 **CD 20** Answer the questions about you.

1. Are you American?

   <u>No, I'm not.</u>

2. Do you speak French?

   _____

3. Are you French?

   _____

4. Do you work in a hotel?

   _____

5. Are you a teacher?

   _____

6. Do you like learning English?

   _____

7. Do your parents speak English?

   _____

## 4 am/is/are, do/does

Complete the sentences with *am*, *is*, *are*, *do*, or *does*.

1. I _____ an accountant.

2. _____ he like his job?

3. Where _____ they live?

4. _____ New York exciting?

5. Why _____ you want to learn English?

6. We _____ American.

7. What _____ he do on weekends?

## 5 Making negatives

Complete the sentences with a negative.

1. I like swimming, but I <u>don't like tennis</u> .

2 I like coffee, but I _____

   _____ .

3. We like playing tennis, but we _____

   _____ .

4. Sue likes cats, but she _____

   _____ .

5. I speak French, but I _____

   _____ .

6. Tom speaks Spanish, but he _____

   _____ .

7. Mr. and Mrs. Green have a son, but they

   _____

# Adverbs of frequency

## 6 Position of adverbs

Put the words in the correct order to make sentences.

1. always / Canada / to / the / go / we / spring / in

    _____

2. stay / hotel / a / usually / we / in

    _____

3. plane / sometimes / by / go / we

    _____

4. sometimes / bus / go / we / by

    _____

5. children / with / never / our / us / come

    _____

6. we / restaurant / go / a / often / Fridays / to / on

    _____

    _____

## 7 Questions about you

1. **CD 21** Answer the questions about you. Use an adverb of frequency in your answer.

    1. How do you come to school?
       *I usually walk.*

    2. What's the first thing you do in the morning?

       _____

    3. Do you have tea or coffee for breakfast?

       _____

    4. What do you do in the evenings?

       _____

    5. What do you do on Sundays?

       _____

    6. Where do you go on vacation?

       _____

    7. Do you have a winter vacation?

       _____

    8. What does your family do in the summer?
       We _____

2. Answer the questions about you. Use the phrases in the box to help you.

    > every morning/evening
    > every day
    > every (Friday)
    > once a week
    > three or four times a year
    > never

    1. How often do you go swimming?      *About once a week.*
    2. How often do you eat in restaurants?   _____
    3. How often do you take a shower?      _____
    4. How often do you go shopping?       _____
    5. How often do you read a newspaper?    _____
    6. How often do you go to the movies?    _____

## 8 Listening – My favorite season

**CD 22** Listen to Brett. Correct the text. There are five mistakes.

# My favorite season

Brett is from the Northern region of the United States. They have cool summers, but they often go to the sea to sunbathe and swim. His favorite season is fall. He likes walking and taking photographs in the Rocky Mountains. It's a beautiful place.

## Prepositions of time

### 9  *in, on, at*

Complete the sentences with *in, on,* or *at.*

1. _____ summer I play tennis _____
   Sundays.
2. The train leaves Tokyo _____ 4 P.M.
3. He likes playing football _____ weekends.
4. My brother's birthday is _____ March.
5. They often eat in a restaurant _____
   Fridays.
6. Vancouver is very cold _____ the winter.

## Vocabulary

### 10  Opposite verbs

1  Match a verb in **A** with its opposite in **B.**

| A | B |
|---|---|
| 1. love | a. close |
| 2. start | b. relax |
| 3. come | c. hate |
| 4. open | d. go |
| 5. leave | e. finish |
| 6. get up | f. arrive |
| 7. work | g. be early |
| 8. be late | h. go to bed |

2  Complete the sentences with the opposite verb in the correct form.

1. Sally hates George, but she _loves_
   Thomas.
2. The bank opens at 8:00 in the morning and
   _____ at 6:00 in the afternoon.
3. The movie starts at 7:15 and _____
   at 10:00.
4. I get up at 6:30 and _____ at 10:30
   on weekdays.
5. She _____ to work at 8:30 in the morning
   and comes home at 6:00.
6. John is often late for school, but I _____ .
7. The train leaves Boston at 5:30 P.M. and
   _____ in New York at 9:15 P.M.
8. I work eight hours a day, so I always
   _____ in the evening.

## Check it

### 11  Translation

Translate these sentences.

1. I always work hard. _____
2. I like helping people. _____
3. How do you travel to work? _____
4. I think he likes playing
   computer games. _____
5. I like fall best. _____
6. **A** I'm sorry I'm late. _____
   **B** That's OK. _____
7. **A** It's very hot in here. _____
   **B** Really? I'm pretty cold. _____

### 12  Listening – Excuse me!

**CD 23** Listen and match the conversations and photos.

a. ☐

b. ☐

c. ☐ TICK

1. **A** Excuse me! Is your name Estella?
   **B** Pardon?
   **A** Is your name Estella?
   **B** No, it isn't.
   **A** Oh, I'm sorry!
   **B** That's OK.

2. **A** I'm sorry I'm late!
   **B** Don't worry. The movie doesn't
   start until eight o'clock.

3. **A** Excuse me! What does this
   word mean?
   **B** I'm sorry, I don't know!
   **A** Thanks anyway.

# 5 Where do you live?

**Grammar:** *there is/are, some/any*
• Prepositions; *this/that/these/those*
**Vocabulary:** Rooms and activities •
Directions 1

## *there is/are, some/any –* prepositions

### 1 Describing a room

Look at the picture of Suzie's bedroom. Are the sentences true (✓) or false (✗)?

1. ☐ There's a chair in front of the desk.
2. ☐ There are some flowers in the bedroom.
3. ☐ There's a mirror on the wall next to the window.
4. ☐ There aren't any plants.
5. ☐ There are some magazines under the table.
6. ☐ There's a lamp next to the bed.
7. ☐ There's a plant next to the door.
8. ☐ There's a photo on the table, in front of the flowers.
9. ☐ There's a bag on the chair.
10. ☐ There are some pictures on the wall.

### 2 Questions and answers

1 Look at the picture of Suzie's bedroom. Complete the questions and answers.

1. **A** Is there a computer?
   **B** Yes, *there is.* It's *on* the desk.
2. **A** _____ there any photos?
   **B** No, _____.
3. **A** Is _____ bag?
   **B** Yes, _____. It's _____ the chair.
4. **A** _____ plant?
   **B** No, _____.
5. **A** _____ flowers?
   **B** Yes, _____. They're _____ the table.
6. **A** _____ magazines?
   **B** Yes, _____. They're _____ the table.

2 Look at the picture again. Complete the conversations.

1. **A** Is there a computer?
   **B** Yes, *there is* _____.
   **A** Where *is it* _____?
   **B** It's *on the desk* _____.
2. **A** Is there a rug?
   **B** Yes, _____.
   **A** Where _____?
   **B** It's _____ the bed.
3. **A** Are there any pictures?
   **B** Yes, _____.
   **A** Where _____?
   **B** They're _____.
4. **A** Are there _____ books?
   **B** Yes, _____.
   **A** Where _____?
   **B** They're _____ the desk _____ the computer.
5. **A** _____ mirror?
   **B** Yes, _____.
   **A** Where _____?
   **B** It's _____ the wall _____ the door.

# Sandy Beach Villa

Come and stay in this beautiful beach house in the Hamptons. It has three comfortable bedrooms with beautiful views and two bathrooms. There's a big kitchen and a living room with large windows. There's a digital TV and music system, and a dishwasher. The house has a private pool and it is on the beach.

This is the perfect place for a relaxing family vacation!

Call (631) 366-7212 or write to the e-mail address below.

◆ **COMFORTABLE BEACH HOUSE** ◆ **BEAUTIFUL VIEWS**
◆ **ON THE BEACH** ◆ **POOL**

sandybeach@hamptons.net

## 3 The perfect place for a vacation

1 **CD 24** Read the advertisement. Complete Paul and Jenny's conversation with the correct form of *there is/are*.

**Jenny** Look at this place in the Hamptons. Isn't it beautiful?

**Paul** Yes, it is. But how big is it? How many bedrooms (1)_____ _____?

**Jenny** (2)_____ _____ three. And (3)_____ _____ two bathrooms!

**Paul** Great! What about the kitchen? And (4)_____ _____ a dishwasher?

**Jenny** Yes, (5)_____ _____ . The kitchen's big and (6)_____ _____ large windows in the living room.

**Paul** Nice. (7)_____ _____ a pool?

**Jenny** Yes, (8)_____ _____ . And, listen to this! It's on the beach.

**Paul** That's great for the children. When do we want to go there?

**Jenny** July, I think.

**Paul** OK. (9)_____ _____ a phone number in the advertisement?

**Jenny** Yes, (10)_____ _____ . And (11)_____ an e-mail address, too.

**Paul** Great!

2 Complete the sentences about Sandy Beach Villa with *some*, *any*, *a*, or *an*.

1. Is there **a**_____ bathroom?
2. There are _____ beautiful views.
3. The beach house has _____ digital TV and _____ digital music system, too.
4. Does the kitchen have _____ dishwasher?
5. There are _____ large windows in the living room.
6. Are there _____ comfortable armchairs in the living room?
7. There's _____ pool in the backyard.
8. On the beach there's _____ small boat.
9. Are there _____ good restaurants near the beach house?
10. There's _____ phone number and _____ e-mail address, too.

## 4 Short answers

Answer the questions about your school and your town.

1. Is there a cafeteria in your school?
   **Yes, there is.**_____
2. Is there a language laboratory? _____
3. Is there a library? _____
4. Are there any computers? _____
5. Are there any bookshelves in your classroom?

   _____
6. Is there a movie theater near your house? _____
7. Are there any parks in your town? _____

# this/that/these/those

## 5 *this* or *that*?

Match the conversations and pictures.

1. ☐ **A** Do you like this photograph?
   **B** Yes, I do. It's nice.
2. ☐ **A** Do you like that picture?
   **B** No, I don't. It's ugly.
3. ☐ **A** How much is this camera?
   **B** It's $250.
4. ☐ **A** How much is that TV?
   **B** It's $399.

## 6 *these* or *those*?

Match the conversations and pictures.

1. ☐ **A** How much are these chairs?
   **B** They're $250 each.
2. ☐ **A** Look at those chairs.
   **B** They're nice.
3. ☐ **A** Look at those children!
   **B** They're Anna's sons.
4. ☐ **A** These are my children.
   **B** They're beautiful.

## 7 *this/these*, *it/they*

Complete the sentences with *this*, *these*, *it*, or *they*.

1. **A** Bob, **this** is my mother.
   **B** Hello, Mrs. Smith.
2. Take _____ bags into the kitchen.
3. I don't like _____ music.
4. **A** Is _____ book Yukio's?
   **B** Yes, _____ is.
5. **A** Are _____ books Tanita's?
   **B** Yes, _____ are.
6. **A** How much are _____ cups?
   **B** They're very cheap.
7. **A** _____ exercise is very easy.
   **B** No, _____ isn't.
   _____'s very hard!

## 8 *that/those*, *it/they*

Complete the sentences with *that*, *those*, *it*, or *they*.

1. Is _____ your brother over there?
2. Look at _____ beautiful flowers!
3. What's _____ in your bag?
4. **A** Is _____ house Jan's?
   **B** Yes, _____ is.
5. **A** Are _____ boys your brothers?
   **B** Yes, _____ are.
6. **A** How much is _____ ?
   **B** _____'s $350.
7. **A** Do you like _____ shoes?
   **B** No, I don't. _____'re ugly.

# Vocabulary

## 9 Rooms and activities

1 Look at the picture and write the words in the correct place.

| living room | coffee table | window | toilet | yard |
| bedroom | refrigerator | sofa | bed | bookshelves |
| stove | bathtub | closet | bathroom | kitchen |
| armchair | cabinets | shower | dishwasher | mirror |

| ❶ bed | ❺ _____ | ❾ _____ | ⓭ _____ | ⓱ _____ |
| 2 _____ | ❻ _____ | ❿ _____ | 14 _____ | 18 _____ |
| ❸ _____ | ❼ _____ | ⓫ _____ | ⓯ _____ | ⓳ _____ |
| ❹ _____ | ❽ _____ | ⓬ _____ | ⓰ _____ | ⓴ _____ |

2 Match a verb in **A** with a word or phrase in **B**.

| A | B |
|---|---|
| 1. listen | a. my hair |
| 2. cook | b. a shower |
| 3. wash | c. to music |
| 4. read | d. dressed |
| 5. go | e. a book |
| 6. take | f. my homework |
| 7. get | g. to bed |
| 8. do | h. dinner |

3 Where do you do the things in Exercise 2? Write sentences.

1. **I listen to music in the living room.**
2. _____
3. _____
4. _____
5. _____
6. _____
7. _____
8. _____

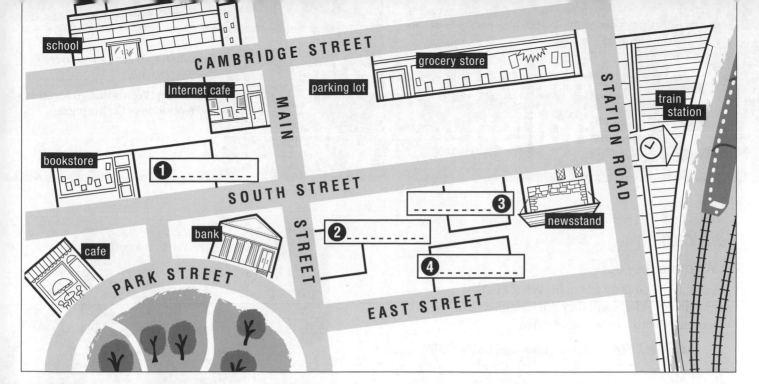

school · CAMBRIDGE STREET · grocery store · parking lot · Internet cafe · MAIN · STATION ROAD · train station · bookstore · 1 _____ · SOUTH STREET · 3 _____ · newsstand · STREET · 2 _____ · bank · 4 _____ · cafe · PARK STREET · EAST STREET

# Check it

## 10 Listening – Directions 1

1 **CD 25** Look at the map. Listen and follow the directions. Write the places on the map.

1. Start at the Internet cafe. Where are you? _____
2. Start at the bookstore. Where are you? _____
3. Start at the train station. Where are you? _____
4. Start at the school. Where are you? _____

2 **CD 26** Look at the map. Complete the conversations.

1. **Start at the school.**

   **A** _____ me. Is there a grocery store _____
   _____?

   **B** Yes. Go _____ ahead and it's on the
   _____.

   **A** Is it _____?

   **B** No, just five minutes, that's _____.

2. **Start at the bookstore.**

   **A** Excuse me. _____ _____ a bank near here?

   **C** Yes. It's _____ _____ Street. Go
   _____ _____ and take the first street on
   the _____ . It's on the _____.

3. **Start at the movie theater.**

   **A** _____ _____ . Is there a drugstore
   _____ here?

   **D** Yes. _____ the first street _____ the
   _____ . It's _____ _____ Street and it's
   on the _____.

   **A** Thanks a _____.

## 11 Translation

Translate these sentences.

1. There's a telephone next to the lamp.

   _____

2. **A** Is there a television on the table?
   **B** No, thcrc isn't.

   _____

   _____

3. **A** Are there any flowers in the living room?
   **B** Yes, there are.

   _____

   _____

4. There are some glasses in the cabinet.

   _____

5. How many rooms are there in your house?

   _____

6. **A** Excuse me. Is there a drugstore near here?
   **B** Yes, there is.

   _____

   _____

7. Go straight ahead, and take the first street on the left.

   _____

   _____

8. It's on the right, next to the cafe.

   _____

# 6 Can you speak English?

**Grammar:** *can/can't • was/were • could/couldn't*
**Vocabulary:** Words that go together • Prepositions • On the phone

## can/can't

### 1 What can they do?

Look at the table on the right. What can the people do? What can't they do? Complete the sentences with *can* or *can't* + verb.

1. Tiago **can't play** the guitar and he **can't play** the piano.
2. Tiago _____ a motorcycle and he _____ a car.
3. Tiago _____ a computer, but he _____ a computer.
4. James _____ a car, but he _____ a motorcycle.
5. Only So-young _____ the piano.
6. Only James _____ .
7. So-young and James can't _____ , but Daniela and Tiago can.
8. Nobody _____ .
9. Everybody _____ .

| | Tiago | James | Daniela | So-young |
|---|---|---|---|---|
| **play the guitar** | ✗ | ✗ | ✗ | ✗ |
| **play the piano** | ✗ | ✗ | ✗ | ✓ |
| **use a computer** | ✓ | ✓ | ✓ | ✓ |
| **program a computer** | ✗ | ✓ | ✗ | ✗ |
| **ride a motorcycle** | ✓ | ✗ | ✓ | ✗ |
| **drive a car** | ✓ | ✓ | ✓ | ✗ |

### 2 What can you do?

**CD 27** Complete the questions with *can* and a verb from the box. Then match the questions and answers.

    play (x2)   speak   ride   use   cook   drive

1. [f] **Can** you **play** the piano?
2. [ ] _____ you _____ any other languages?
3. [ ] _____ you _____ the guitar?
4. [ ] _____ you _____ a motorcycle?
5. [ ] _____ you _____ a computer?
6. [ ] _____ you _____ Italian food?
7. [ ] _____ you _____ a car?

a. Yes, I can. French and Spanish.
b. Yes, I can, but I can't program one.
c. No, I can't. I think they're dangerous.
d. No, I can't, but I love eating it.
e. No, I can't, but I can play the piano.
f. Yes, I can. I like playing Mozart.
g. Yes, I can. I have a Volkswagen.

## was/were

### 3 Present or past?

Complete the sentences with *am, is, are, was,* or *were.*

1. The homework **was** very difficult yesterday.
2. Hello, everybody! I _____ sorry I _____ late!
3. **A** Where _____ you born?
   **B** I _____ born in Taiwan.
4. **A** Where _____ your sister born?
   **B** She _____ born in Taiwan, too.
5. The weather _____ beautiful today. It _____ awful yesterday.
6. The children _____ very tired today. They _____ at a party last night.
7. I could play chess when I _____ five.
8. We _____ married when I _____ eighteen and Roger _____ twenty.

## 4 Listening – How much was it before?

1 Label this picture using the words in the box.

~~camera~~    glasses    lamps
television    table

2 **CD 28** Listen to the conversations. Write the prices on the picture.

3 Write the first two conversations.

1. **A** How much _____ the camera?
   **B** _____ only $_____ .
   **A** How much _____ it before?
   **B** It _____ $_____ .
   **A** Well, what a bargain!

2. **A** How _____ _____ the glasses?
   **B** They're _____ .
   **A** _____ ?
   **B** _____ .
   **A** _____ !

SALE! SALE! SALE!

1 camera
Only $60
Was $ 110

3
Only $
Were $99.99

2
Only $39.99
Were $

5
Only $
Was $500

4
Only $69.99
Was $

## 5 Questions and short answers

1 **CD 29** Read about Greg and Sofia.

2 Answer the questions about Greg and Sofia's day yesterday.

1. Was Sofia at work yesterday morning? _Yes, she was._____
2. Was Greg at work yesterday morning? _____
3. Where were Greg and Sofia at seven o'clock yesterday morning? _____
4. Was Sofia in the bathroom at twenty-five to eight yesterday morning? _____
5. Was Greg in the kitchen at 11:15? _____
6. Was Sofia at school at four o'clock in the afternoon? _____
7. Where were Sofia and Greg at five o'clock yesterday afternoon? _____
8. Where was Greg at 5:45 in the afternoon? _____
9. Was Sofia at home at seven o'clock yesterday evening? _____
10. Where were they at 8:30 last night? _____

## A typical day for Greg and Sofia

Greg is a waiter and Sofia is a teacher's assistant in an elementary school. Sofia gets up at 7:30 a.m. and takes a shower. She has breakfast at 8:00, and then she walks to school. She starts work at 8:40.

Greg gets up at 11:00 and takes a shower. He doesn't have breakfast because he has lunch at 12:00. He leaves home at 5:30 and goes to work by bus. He starts work at 6:00.

Sofia finishes work at 3:45 and walks home. Sofia and Greg have a very early dinner at 5:00. They cook and they chat until Greg leaves for work. Sofia relaxes at home until about 7:30. Then she goes to Greg's restaurant for an hour. She goes home at about 9:00, watches TV until 10:30, then she goes to bed.

Greg arrives home at about 1:30 in the morning. He has a glass of milk and goes to bed at 2:00.

## could/couldn't

### 6 When I was three, I could . . .

1 Write three things you could do when you were three.

1. *I could run.* _____

2. _____

3. _____

4. _____

2 Write three things you can do now that you couldn't do when you were three.

1. *I couldn't swim when I was three, but I can now.* _____

2. _____

3. _____

4. _____

3 Write two things you couldn't do when you were three and you still can't do.

1. *I couldn't ski when I was three and I still can't.* _____

2. _____

3. _____

## Vocabulary

### 7 Words that go together

1 Match a verb in **A** with a word or phrase in **B**.

| A | B |
|---|---|
| 1. stay | a. fluently |
| 2. ask | b. the answer |
| 3. know | c. a question |
| 4. start | d. a phone call |
| 5. go | e. in a hotel |
| 6. get up | f. work |
| 7. live | g. home |
| 8. speak English | h. pictures |
| 9. make | i. early |
| 10. paint | j. alone |

2 Complete the conversations with a word or words from Exercise 1 in the correct form.

1. **A** Maria! Do you *know the answer?* _____

   **B** I'm sorry. I can't remember the question!

2. **A** Your son is a very good artist.

   **B** Thank you very much. He could _____
   when he was just three.

3. **A** Can you play tennis at nine o'clock on Sunday?

   **B** I'm sorry. I never _____ on
   Sundays. I stay in bed until eleven.

4. **A** What time do you _____
   every day?

   **B** I'm always in the office and at my desk at 9:00.

5. **A** Is your friend English?

   **B** No, she isn't, but she _____ .

6. **A** Does your sister _____ ?

   **B** No, she doesn't. She lives with two friends.

7. **A** Do you want to go to the movies after work?

   **B** No, thanks. I'm really tired. I just want to
   _____ .

8. **A** Where do you stay when you go on vacation?

   **B** We usually _____ by the sea.

## 8 Prepositions

Complete the sentences with a preposition from the box.

| by | with | of | in | on | at | to |

1. I was _____ Sergio's party _____ Saturday.

2. Luisa lives _____ home _____ her parents.

3. Tom is _____ the backyard _____ his friend Sam.

4. I go _____ work _____ bus and I'm _____ work until 5:30 P.M. every day.

5. She was _____ the movies _____ her boyfriend _____ Friday evening.

6. Tim was born _____ San Diego _____ 1981.

7. **A** Can you help me _____ my homework?
   **B** _____ course I can; give it _____ me.

8. Look _____ this photo _____ my girlfriend. Isn't she beautiful?

# Check it

## 9 Translation

Translate these sentences.

1. We can read, but we can't write.

   _____

2. **A** I can draw very well.
   **B** No, you can't!

   _____

3. **A** Can you dance?
   **B** Yes, I can.

   _____

4. What month was it last month?

   _____

5. Were you in the U.S. in 2001?

   _____

6. **A** Could you swim when you were five?
   **B** No, I couldn't.

   _____

7. **A** Hello. Can I speak to Jo, please?
   **B** This is Jo.

   _____

8. Can I take a message?

   _____

## 10 Listening – On the phone

**CD 30** Listen to the telephone conversations. Complete the messages and write the information.

1. **Paul and Jane**

   "Can you come _____ ?"

   DAY: _____

   TIME: _____

2. **John and Barry**

   "Can you _____ ?"

   DAY: _____

   TIME: _____

3. **Meg and Kate**

   "Can you _____ ?"

   DAY: _____

   TIME: _____

# 7 Then and now

## Past Simple 1

### 1 Regular verbs

Match a line in **A** with a line in **B**. Put the verb in **A** into the Present Simple and the verb in **B** into the Past Simple.

**A**

1. I usually **work** (work) eight hours a day, but ...
2. Jerry usually _____ (drive) to work, but ...
3. Max usually _____ (watch) TV in the evenings, but ...
4. Ann and Max usually _____ (play) tennis on weekends, but ...
5. It usually _____ (snow) a lot in winter, but ...
6. Ann, Max, Jerry, and I usually _____ (go) the beach in August, but ...

**B**

a. ... last summer we _____ (stay) in a hotel in the mountains.
b. ... last weekend they _____ (go) sailing.
c. ... yesterday I _____ (start) work at 9:00 A.M. and _____ (finish) at 9:00 P.M.
d. ... last year it _____ (rain) for three months.
e. ... yesterday he _____ (walk).
f. ... yesterday evening he _____ (listen) to music.

## 2 Yes/No questions and short answers

Write questions and answers about the people in Exercise 1.

1. **A** Do you usually work eight hours a day?
   **B** Yes, *I do.*
   **A** Did *you work eight hours yesterday?*
   **B** No, *I didn't. I worked twelve hours.*

2. **A** Does Jerry usually drive to work?
   **B** Yes, _____.
   **A** Did he _____ yesterday?
   **B** No, _____.

3. **A** Does Max usually watch TV in the evenings?
   **B** Yes, _____.
   **A** Did he _____ last night?
   **B** No, _____.

4. **A** Do Ann and Max usually play tennis on weekends?
   **B** _____
   **A** _____
   **B** _____

5. **A** Does it usually snow a lot in winter?
   **B** _____
   **A** _____
   **B** _____

6. **A** Do you, Max, Ann, and Jerry usually go to the beach in August?
   **B** Yes, we _____
   **A** _____
   **B** _____

## 3 had/did, was/were

**CD 31** Complete Miguel and Emma's conversation with *had*, *did*, *was*, or *were*.

**M** I (1)_____ my English exam last week.

**E** Oh, really? (2)_____ it difficult?

**M** Yes, it (3)_____ very difficult.

**E** (4)_____ you worried?

**M** Of course! All my classmates (5)_____ worried. We could not sleep the night before!

**E** (6)_____ you pass the exam, then?

**M** Yes! We all (7)_____. We (8)_____ a party last night! We (9)_____ so happy!

## 4 Irregular verbs

**CD 32** Complete the table with the verbs in the box. Write the Past Simple forms.

| | | | | |
|---|---|---|---|---|
| ~~begin~~ | ~~start~~ | visit | write | leave |
| win | buy | do | see | enjoy |
| go | take | paint | have | drive |
| speak | travel | come | stay | meet |

| Regular verbs | | Irregular verbs | |
|---|---|---|---|
| **Infinitive** | **Past Simple** | **Infinitive** | **Past Simple** |
| start | started | begin | began |
| _____ | _____ | _____ | _____ |
| _____ | _____ | _____ | _____ |
| _____ | _____ | _____ | _____ |
| _____ | _____ | _____ | _____ |
| | | _____ | _____ |
| | | _____ | _____ |
| | | _____ | _____ |
| | | _____ | _____ |
| | | _____ | _____ |
| | | _____ | _____ |
| | | _____ | _____ |

## 5 Negatives and affirmatives

Complete the sentences with the affirmative form of the verb.

1. I didn't go to New York, I **went** to Chicago.
2. We didn't meet Jerry, we _____ Max.
3. He didn't leave last Tuesday, he _____ last Thursday.
4. We didn't see you, but we _____ Ann.
5. They didn't buy a Volvo, they _____ a Honda.
6. You didn't know the answer, but Elsa _____ the answer.
7. I didn't lose my passport, I _____ my ticket.
8. We didn't have cake, we _____ fruit.
9. He didn't write a letter, he _____ a postcard.
10. The movie didn't begin at 6:30 P.M., it _____ at 7:30 P.M.

## 6 Making questions

Put the words in the correct order to make questions. Then write true answers.

1. school / did / when / start / you / ?
   **When did you start school?**
   **When I was six. In 1985.**

2. morning / you / time / get / up / what / this / did / ?
   _____
   _____

3. dinner / night / have / what / you / last / for / did / ?
   _____
   _____

4. did / train / last / you / by / when / travel / ?
   _____
   _____

5. do / what / Sunday / you / last / did / ?
   _____
   _____

6. vacation / did / summer / on / go / where / last / you / ?
   _____
   _____

7. visit / you / art gallery / an / last / did / when / ?
   _____
   _____

8. come / today / you / how / school / did / to / ?
   _____
   _____

# Present Simple and Past Simple

## 7 A biography

### 1 Complete the text using the correct form of the verbs in the box.

**British artist, Lucian Freud** born 1922

Lucian Freud was born in Berlin, Germany, but now he (1) __lives__ in London. He (2) __moved__ to Britain in 1933 when Hitler (3) _____ to Germany. His grandfather (4) _____ Sigmund Freud, the famous psychoanalyst.

| come |
|---|
| ~~live~~ |
| be |
| ~~move~~ |

He is 86 years old now, but he still (5) _____ every day. He (6) _____ painting portraits of people. He (7) _____ on a painting for eight or nine months.

| work |
|---|
| paint |
| love |

He (8) _____ at the Central School of Arts in London in 1938 and 1939. Then he (9) _____ a sailor in World War II, but he (10) _____ to the hospital soon after. In 1942, he (11) _____ painting. He (12) _____ a prize at the Festival of Britain in 1951 and he (13) _____ the Queen in 2001.

| become |
|---|
| study |
| win |
| go |
| start |
| paint |

He (14) _____ married twice, but now he (15) _____ alone. He (16) _____ very often. His paintings (17) _____ for a lot of money and people (18) _____ he is Britain's best living painter.

| live |
|---|
| not go out |
| sell |
| be |
| think |

### 2 Write short answers to the questions.

1. Was Lucian Freud born in Britain?
   __No, he wasn't.__

2. Did he go to Britain in 1933?
   __Yes, he did.__

3. Was his father the famous psychoanalyst Sigmund Freud?
   _____

4. Is Lucian Freud 90 years old?
   _____

5. Does he still paint?
   _____

6. Does he love painting cats?
   _____

7. Did he study at the Central School of Arts in 1939?
   _____

8. Did he become a sailor in World War I?
   _____

9. Did he paint the Queen?
   _____

10. Was he married?
    _____

### 3 Write questions for these answers.

1. __Where was Lucian Freud born?__
   In Berlin.

2. _____
   In London.

3. _____
   He went there in 1933.

4. _____
   He's an artist.

5. _____
   In 1942.

6. _____
   in 2001?
   The Queen.

7. _____
   sell for?
   A lot of money.

# Vocabulary

## 8 Parts of speech

1 Write the correct part of speech next to each word in the box.

*n* = noun    *v* = verb    *adj* = adjective
*prep* = preposition

| | | |
|---|---|---|
| _adj_ nice | ___ enjoy | ___ waiter |
| ___ vacation | ___ new | ___ on |
| ___ party | ___ in | ___ relax |
| ___ see | ___ warm | ___ famous |
| ___ near | ___ earn | ___ win |

2 Complete the sentences with a word from Exercise 1. Change the verb forms if necessary.

1. My aunt lives in a *(adj)* **nice**___, old house *(prep)* **near**___ the ocean.

2. Did you *(v)* _____ Frank's *(adj)* _____ car this morning? It's red.

3. I play tennis with her *(prep)* _____ Sundays and she always *(v)* _____.

4. I *(v)* _____ and watched television yesterday evening. It was so *(adj)* _____ in front of the fire.

5. I saw a *(adj)* _____ movie star at Peter's *(n)* _____.

6. He worked as a *(n)* _____ until he died, and he only *(v)* _____ $15,000 a year.

7. They took a *(n)* _____ *(prep)* _____ Mexico and they *(v)* _____ it very much.

# Check it

## 9 Translation

Translate these sentences.

1. She worked at a radio station.

_____

2. **A** Does she live in California?
   **B** Yes, she does.

_____

3. She didn't have any money.

_____

4. **A** When did you last take a vacation?
   **B** Last August.

_____

5. What did you do last week?

_____

6. I married Ivan on July 12, 2002.

_____

## 10 Listening – Douglas Corrigan's amazing journey

**CD 33** Listen and put the pictures in the correct order, 1–7.

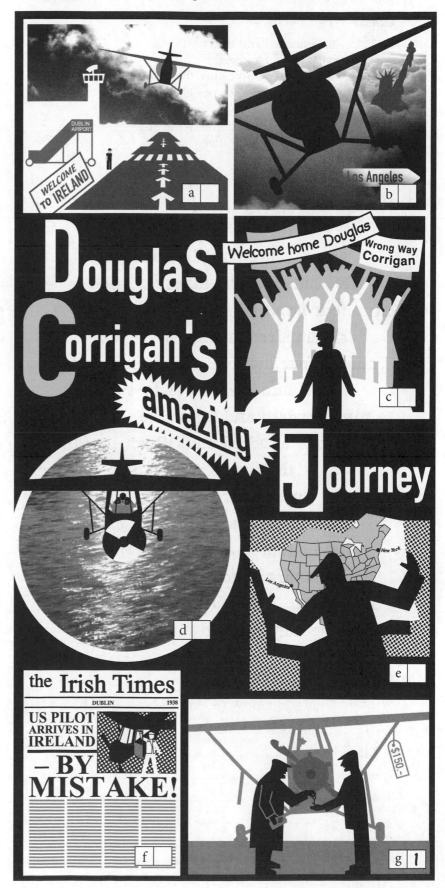

# Numbers

## 11 100–1,000

**CD 34** Listen and repeat.

| | |
|---|---|
| 130 | one hundred and thirty |
| 508 | five hundred and eight |
| 285 | two hundred and eighty-five |
| 678 | six hundred and seventy-eight |
| 300 | three hundred |
| 793 | seven hundred and ninety-three |
| 415 | four hundred and fifteen |
| 1,000 | one thousand |

## 12 Matching numbers and words

Match the numbers and the words.

945    three hundred and ten

five hundred and ninety    800

115    four hundred and seventy-one    999

six hundred and three    508

144    four hundred and twenty-five

eight hundred and sixty-two

nine hundred and forty-five    590

603    one hundred and fifteen    616

eight hundred    310

734    one hundred and forty-four

five hundred and eight    425

two hundred and thirty-eight

seven hundred and thirty-four    238

862    471    six hundred and sixteen

nine hundred and ninety-nine

## 13 Writing numbers and words

1 Write the numbers in words.

1. 411    four hundred and eleven _____
2. 145    _____
3. 610    _____
4. 890    _____
5. 387    _____
6. 150    _____
7. 532    _____

2 Answer the questions. Write the numbers in words.

1. How many days are there in a year?

   _____

2. How many minutes are there in two hours?

   _____

3. How many pages are there in this book?

   _____

4. How many students are there in your school?

   _____

5. How many weeks are there in four years?

   _____

6. How many cents are there in $4.73?

   _____

# Prepositions

## 14 about, after, for ...

Complete the sentences with a preposition from the box.

| about | after | for | in | to | over | with | at |
|---|---|---|---|---|---|---|---|

1. My family left San Francisco and moved ___to___ a small town.
2. People all _____ the world speak English.
3. Did you speak _____ the teacher _____ the homework?
4. What do you know _____ George Washington?
5. Peter stayed _____ his grandmother _____ two weeks.
6. I often think _____ the day we met.
7. New Year's Day is one week _____ Christmas Day.
8. We arrived _____ the airport _____ New York _____ 5:45 A.M.
9. Here's the mail carrier _____ a letter _____ you.
10. Speak _____ me in English. It's good practice _____ us.

# 8 A date to remember

**Grammar:** Past Simple 2 • Past time expressions • *ago*
**Vocabulary:** Nouns and verbs • A short story • Special occasions

## Past Simple 2

### 1 Regular and irregular verbs

Read about Alexander Graham Bell. Put the verbs into the Past Simple.

### Alexander Graham Bell (1847–1922)

#### Inventor of the telephone

Alexander Graham Bell (1) **was** (be) born in Edinburgh, Scotland. His mother (2) _____ (be) deaf, so all his life he (3) _____ (want) to help his mother hear and speak. Alexander was very clever. He (4) _____ (can) read and write when he was very young, and he (5) _____ (finish) school when he was 14. At 14 he also (6) _____ (invent) a "speaking" machine with his brother.

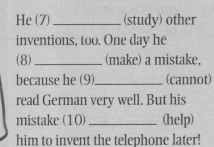

He (7) _____ (study) other inventions, too. One day he (8) _____ (make) a mistake, because he (9)_____ (cannot) read German very well. But his mistake (10) _____ (help) him to invent the telephone later!

In 1871 he (11) _____ (leave) Scotland and (12) _____ (go) to Boston, in the U.S., to teach deaf children to speak. He (13) _____ (meet) his assistant Thomas Watson and he (14) _____ (continue) his experiments.

On March 10, 1876, Watson and Bell (15) _____ (be) in different rooms with their machines. Then Watson (16) _____ (hear) Bell's voice from the machine. It (17) _____ (say) "Mr. Watson, come here. I want you!" And so Alexander Graham Bell (18) _____ (become) the inventor of the telephone at the age of 29. Two years later, there were telephones all over the U.S.

### 2 Making negatives

Correct the sentences about Alexander Graham Bell.

1. Alexander Graham Bell was American.
   **He wasn't American. He was Scottish.**

2. He wanted to help his mother to see.
   _____
   _____

3. He finished school at eighteen.
   _____
   _____

4. He invented a "writing" machine.
   _____
   _____

5. He made a mistake reading French.
   _____
   _____

6. He went to the U.S. in 1877.
   _____

7. Bell heard Watson's voice from the machine.
   _____
   _____

8. He invented the telephone at 59.
   _____
   _____

## 3 Negative short forms

**CD 35** Write the short forms of the negative verbs.

1. She did not see me.

   **She didn't see me.**

2. I did not go to school on Monday.

   _____

3. Our teacher did not come to school today.

   _____

4. Tina was not in Seattle last month.

   _____

5. They were not at home.

   _____

6. Larry could not read until he was eight.

   _____

## 4 Affirmatives and negatives

Make the affirmative verbs negative. Make the negative verbs affirmative.

1. She drove to work.

   **She didn't drive to work.**

2. I didn't know the answer.

   **I knew the answer.**

3. My aunt gave me a birthday present.

   _____

4. It didn't rain a lot during our vacation.

   _____

5. I didn't drink the coffee, but I ate the sandwich.

   _____

6. She didn't bring a bottle of water.

   _____

7. She wasn't tired, so she didn't go to bed.

   _____

8. He forgot his passport and he lost his plane ticket.

   _____

9. It didn't cost a lot of money.

   _____

10. I didn't have a lot of time, so I didn't go shopping.

    _____

## 5 Past time expressions

1 Number the times in chronological order, 1–6. (1 is nearest in time.)

   ☐ this morning
   ☐ last winter
   ☐ in 1980
   ☐ the day before yesterday
   ☐ last night
   ☐ ten years ago

2 Write sentences about you. Use each of the expressions above once.

   1. **I got up at eight o'clock this morning.**
   2. **I didn't take a shower last night.**
   3. _____
   4. _____
   5. _____
   6. _____
   7. _____
   8. _____

## 6 ago

Rewrite the sentences using *ago*.

1. I saw him last June.

   **I saw him three months ago.**

2. I had breakfast at eight o'clock.

   _____

3. They got married in 1990.

   _____

4. We saw John the day before yesterday.

   _____

5. We met in 1975.

   _____

6. My daughter started school last September.

   _____

7. Mother Teresa died in 1997.

   _____

8. Alice came back from Peru last month.

   _____

9. Their son was born at two o'clock this morning.

   _____

# Vocabulary

## 7 Words that are nouns and verbs

Many words in English are both nouns and verbs. Complete the pairs of sentences with the correct form of a word from the box.

| ~~dance~~ | cook | love | walk | drink |
|-----------|------|------|------|-------|
| watch | paint | mail | visit | |

1. She went to the **dance** on Saturday night and she met Frank.
   The music was wonderful. I **danced** all night long.

2. Can I have a _____ ? I'm really thirsty.
   John never _____ coffee. He doesn't like it.

3. I _____ a meal for ten people yesterday evening.
   **A** What's your job?
   **B** I'm a _____ . I work in a big hotel.

4. We _____ the game on television last night.
   **A** What's the time?
   **B** Sorry. I don't have a _____ .

5. **A** How did you get to work yesterday?
   **B** I _____ .
   We went for a _____ by the lake. It was beautiful.

6. Please give my _____ to your wife and children.
   Anna _____ chocolate ice cream.

7. We really enjoyed our _____ to Boston last weekend.
   When I was in New York last year, I _____ lots of interesting places.

8. I can see the mail carrier. Is there any _____ for me?
   Don't forget to _____ my letter for me!

9. I _____ all the walls in my room blue last weekend.
   What's that in your hair? Is it blue _____ ?

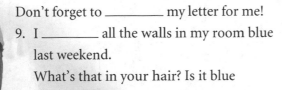

## 8 A crossword puzzle

Complete the puzzle. What is the extra word?

1. When I was a child, I rode to school on this.

2. I don't like reading when I travel by car, but I always read when I travel by _____ .

3. Did you watch the interesting program on _____ last night?

4. I forgot my _____ , so I couldn't take any photographs.

5. A pilot flies a _____ .

6. Most offices, banks, hotels, and schools have them now, but they didn't twenty-five years ago.

7. One hundred years ago, people didn't have one of these in their kitchen to keep food cold.

8. Alexander Graham Bell invented this.

9. Most people now have automatic _____ machines for cleaning their clothes.

10. Mary Anderson invented windshield _____ .

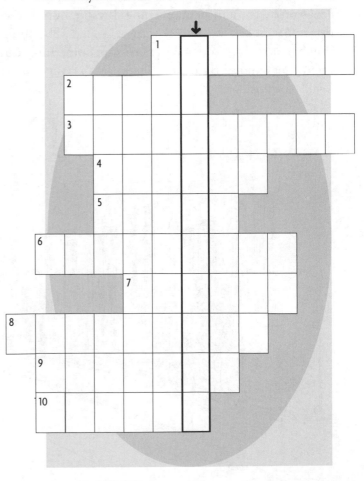

All of these things are _____ .

# The Engagement

## PART 1

My mother never came to meet me at the train station when I arrived from New York. So I always (1) _____ to my mother's house. And so tonight I had time to think. I had some very important news for my mother, but I (2) _____ what to say to her.

I wrote to my mother every week. But it's difficult to (3) _____: "I think Agnes likes me," or "I'm in love with her," or "I think she's in love with me." "I want to ask Agnes (4) _____ ."
Well, I couldn't do it. And yesterday I asked Agnes to marry me, and she said yes.

My mother was a widow. I was her only child—and now (5) _____ and she didn't know. I was ready for a difficult evening. I walked up to the front door. (6) _____ . She smiled and put her arms around me. There was something different about her smile. I thought, "She knows about Agnes!" But I said nothing.

## 9 A short story – *The Engagement*

1  Read part 1 of the short story about Philip. Complete the text with the words in the box.

| | |
|---|---|
| to marry me | write in a letter |
| I was engaged | There was my mother |
| I ran to open it | I had a surprise |
| walked alone from the station | didn't know |

2  Answer the questions.
1. Where did Philip live?
2. Why did he make the trip?
3. How did he get from the station to the house?
4. What news did he have for his mother?
5. Did he have any brothers or sisters?
6. Why did he think that his mother knew about Agnes?
7. Why did he have a surprise in the dining room?
8. What do you think? Was Agnes at the door?

I went into the dining room and here (7) _____ . There were three chairs, three plates, and three glasses. Was Agnes here? Was it a surprise for me? There was a knock at the door. "It's Agnes!" I thought, and (8) _____ .

3 Read part 2 of the story.

# PART 2

But it was Mr. Nixon. He was an old friend of the family.

"Good evening, young man," he said.

"Mr. Nixon is here for dinner, Philip," said my mother. I liked him, but I wasn't very happy to see him tonight because I wanted to talk to my mother. We started our dinner, but we didn't say very much. At the end of the meal, I told my mother that I wanted to go to the post office. I had an important letter to mail.

"A letter to a girl?" laughed Mr. Nixon.

"Yes," I said.

When I got back home, Mr. Nixon was still there.

"Come and sit down, Philip," he said. "Can I talk to you?"

I sat down. "Well, my boy," he said. "I want to marry your mother."

I was surprised.

"I asked her to marry me yesterday, and she said yes. Did she tell you about me in her letters? No? Well, it's difficult to write about that in a letter, of course."

I laughed. "Yes, it is. This is wonderful news."

Then my mother came in, a little red in the face.

It was something new to me that my mother could fall in love. Perhaps, like all sons, I only thought about my own life. So I decided to say nothing about my news. That evening my mother came first for me. I could tell her about Agnes tomorrow.

4 Answer the questions.

1. Who was Mr. Nixon?
2. Why wasn't Philip happy when he saw him?
3. Why did Philip want to go to the post office?
4. Who was the letter for?
5. What did Mr. Nixon tell Philip?
6. Did Philip know about this?
7. What did he think about this news?
8. Did he tell his mother about Agnes that evening?

5 **CD 36** Now read and listen to the complete story.

# Check it

## 10 Translation

Translate these sentences.

1. When were cars invented?

   _____

2. My parents got married thirty years ago.

   _____

3. They got engaged when they were both 25.

   _____

4. I went out with my boyfriend for a year.

   _____

5. Congratulations! When's the big day?

   _____

6. Thank goodness! It's Friday!

   _____

## 11 Listening – Special occasions

**CD 37** Listen to the conversations. Number the occasions in the correct order.

☐ New Year's Eve       ☐ Thanksgiving
☐ birthday              ☐ engagement
☐ Christmas

# 9 Food you like!

**Grammar:** Count and noncount nouns • *Do you like ... ?* • *Would you like ... ?* • *some/any* • *How much/ many ... ?*

**Vocabulary:** Food and drink • In a restaurant

## Count and noncount nouns

### 1 Can you count these?

Are these usually count or noncount nouns? Put *C* or *N*.

1. [N] pasta
2. [ ] money
3. [ ] bread
4. [ ] stamp
5. [ ] juice
6. [ ] apple
7. [ ] hamburger
8. [ ] strawberry
9. [ ] biscuit
10. [ ] fruit
11. [ ] sandwich
12. [ ] cheese
13. [ ] cup
14. [ ] egg

### 2 *a, an,* or *some*?

Complete the sentences with *a, an,* or *some*.

1. Would you like **some** pasta?
2. Would you like _____ juice?
3. Can I have _____ stamps, please?
4. I'd like _____ chicken sandwich and _____ cheese for lunch.
5. Do you want _____ drink?
6. Would you like _____ apple or _____ strawberries?
7. Can I have _____ bread?
8. Can you give me _____ money?
9. I usually have _____ cookie and _____ cup of coffee at 11 A.M.
10. Could you buy _____ fruit when you go to the store?
11. He always has _____ egg for breakfast.

## Do you like ...?

### 3 *like + -ing*

Answer the questions with a word from **A**, a line from **B**, and a line from **C**.

| A | B | C |
|---|---|---|
| love | skiing | crosswords |
| like | looking at | old movies |
| likes | taking | music |
| loves | doing | in the mountains |
| | watching | and windsurfing |
| | sunbathing | computer games |
| | listening to | photographs |
| | playing | paintings |

1. Why does Peter go to Vermont every winter?
   Because he **likes skiing in the mountains** .

2. Why is there a music system in your living room, kitchen, and bedroom?
   Because I _____ .

3. Why does your father buy three newspapers every day?
   Because he _____ .

4. Why do you have a DVD player?
   Because I _____ .

5. Why does Silvia have two cameras?
   Because she _____ .

6. Why do you visit so many art galleries?
   Because I _____ .

7. Why do Ines and Pablo go to the beach on weekends?
   Because they _____ .

8. Why is there a computer in your son's bedroom?
   Because he _____ .

## 4 Likes and dislikes

|  | Lisa likes | Lisa dislikes |
|---|---|---|
| **Sports** | volleyball<br>baseball | football<br>tennis |
| **Food** | Italian<br>Mexican | Chinese |
| **On weekends** | going to restaurants<br>meeting friends | cleaning the house<br>grocery shopping |
| **Movies** | comedies<br>romantic | science fiction |

1 Read the information about Lisa, then complete the questions and answers.

1. What sports **does she like?**
   **Baseball and volleyball.**

2. What kind of food does she like?
   _____

3. _____ doing?
   Going to restaurants and meeting friends.

4. What sort of _____?
   Romantic movies and comedies.

5. _____ Chinese food?
   No, she _____ .

6. _____ watching football?
   _____

7. _____ going to restaurants?
   _____

8. _____ shopping?
   _____

2 Complete the questions, then answer them about you.

1. Do you like **swimming** (swim)?
   **No, I don't.**

2. Do you like _____ (cook)?
   _____

3. Do you like _____ (shop)?
   _____

4. Do you like _____ (play) computer games?
   _____

5. Do you like _____ (do) homework?
   _____

6. Do you like _____ (learn) English?
   _____

# Would you like . . . ?

## 5 I'd like . . .
Match a line in **A** with a line in **B**.

| A | B |
|---|---|
| 1. I'm thirsty. | a. I'd like to go to bed. |
| 2. I'm hungry. | b. I'd like to take some medicine. |
| 3. I'm tired. | c. I'd like to put on my coat. |
| 4. I'm sick. | d. I'd like to go out with my friends. |
| 5. It's Sunday and I'm bored. | e. I'd like to be a millionaire. |
| 6. I don't have any money. | f. I'd like a cold drink. |
| 7. It's winter and I'm cold. | g. I'd like a sandwich. |

## 6 like or would like?
Make sentences with *like* or *'d like*.

1. Jane has all of Eminem's CDs.
   **She likes Eminem.**

2. It's Ann's birthday next week.
   **She'd like some new clothes** for her birthday.

3. Luciana has more than twenty cookbooks.
   _____ cooking.

4. My car is twenty years old!
   _____ a new one.

5. Joe thinks his house is very small.
   _____

6. My children have four cats, three dogs, and a bird.
   _____ animals.

7. There's a good movie on TV tonight.
   _____ watch it.

8. Miwako buys a lot of CDs.
   _____

9. I don't want to go out tonight.
   _____

10. Tom and Mary always take a winter vacation.
    _____

## 7 Ordering a meal in a restaurant
1 Read the menu. Choose what you would like and complete the conversation with the waiter.

**Waiter** Would you like to order?

**You** Yes, please. First, I'd like the _____.
And then I'd like the _____.

**Waiter** Certainly. And would you like some vegetables?

**You** _____.

**Waiter** That's fine. And for dessert?

**You** _____.

**Waiter** Certainly.

# CAFE NOIR

### STARTERS
Vegetable soup

Duck salad

Salmon with toast

Grilled shrimp

❋·❋·❋·❋·❋·❋·❋·❋·❋

### MAIN COURSES
Sirloin steak

Chicken with mushrooms

Fresh tuna steak

Various omelettes

❋·❋·❋·❋·❋·❋·❋·❋·❋

### VEGETABLES
(All our vegetables are fresh and organic)

Rice, potatoes, or french fries

Carrots

Peas

Green salad

❋·❋·❋·❋·❋·❋·❋·❋·❋

### DESSERTS
Fresh fruit salad

Apple pie

Cheesecake

2   Put the words in the correct order to make questions and sentences in a restaurant.

1. coffee / you / like / some / would / ?

   _____

2. order / to / water / you / like / some / would / ?

   _____

   _____

3. water / tap / bottled / or / ?

   _____

4. table / two / a / we'd / for / like

   _____

5. check / have / can / the / we / ?

   _____

6. menu / have / we / the / could / ?

   _____

7. included / service / is / ?

   _____

8. first / soup / I'd / like / the

   _____

9. course / the / the / I'd / chicken / for / main / like

   _____

   _____

10. vegetables / you / what / would / like / ?

   _____

3   **CD 38** Use the sentences in Exercise 2 to complete the conversation.

| | |
|---|---|
| **Waiter** | Good evening, sir. Good evening, madam. |
| **George** | Good evening. (a)_____, please. |
| **Waiter** | Certainly. Is this table all right? |
| **George** | That's fine. (b)_____, please? |
| **Waiter** | Certainly. |
| **Waiter** | Are you ready to order? |
| **George** | Yes. (c)_____. |
| **Linda** | And for me the grilled shrimp. |
| **Waiter** | Yes, madam. |
| **George** | And then (d)_____. |
| **Linda** | And I'd like the tuna. |
| **Waiter** | Certainly, madam. (e)_____? |
| **Linda** | Potatoes and peas, please. |
| **Waiter** | (f)_____? |
| **Linda** | Yes, please. |
| **Waiter** | (g)_____? |
| **Linda** | Bottled, please. |
| **George** | That was delicious! |
| **Waiter** | Thank you very much. (h)_____? |
| **Linda** | Yes. Black, please. |
| **George** | And (i)_____? |
| **Waiter** | Of course. |
| **George** | (j)_____? |
| **Waiter** | No, it isn't, sir. |
| **George** | Can I pay by credit card? |
| **Waiter** | Yes, that's fine. |

## some/any

### 8 some or any?

**1** Complete the sentences with *some* or *any*.

1. I don't have **any** money in my pocket, but I have **some** money in the bank.
2. Are there _____ letters for me this morning?
3. I never have _____ breakfast. I'm not hungry in the morning.
4. You have _____ beautiful pictures in your house.
5. Are you Canadian? I have _____ good friends in Canada.
6. Don't buy _____ bread at the store. There's a lot in the kitchen.
7. Do you have _____ brothers or sisters?
8. There aren't _____ stores in my neighborhood, just a post office and a restaurant.
9. I want _____ cheese. Is there _____ in the refrigerator?
10. _____ people like flying, but other people don't.
11. There was _____ rain during the night.

**2** Complete the sentences with *some* or *any* and a word from the box.

| ~~music~~ | food | gas | stamps |
|-----------|--------|--------|--------|
| books | people | chairs | photos |

1. Would you like to listen to **some music** ? I have a new CD.
2. People couldn't sit down at the party because there weren't _____ .
3. I couldn't take _____ on vacation because my camera broke.
4. We couldn't buy _____ at the grocery store because our money was in the car.
5. I need to put _____ in the car. It's nearly empty.
6. Do you have _____ ? I want to mail this letter.
7. There were _____ very interesting _____ at the party last night.
8. I want _____ from the library.

## How much ... ? and How many ... ?

### 9 How much ... ? or How many ... ?

**CD 39** Complete the questions with *How much ... ?* or *How many ... ?*, then answer them.

1. **How much** homework do you get?
   _____

2. _____ English books do you have?
   _____

3. _____ does a cup of coffee cost?
   _____

4. _____ languages do you speak?
   _____

5. _____ people are there in your class?
   _____

6. _____ weeks' vacation do you have in the summer?
   _____

7. _____ coffee do you drink a day?
   _____

## Check it

### 10 Translation

Translate the sentences.

1. I really like fruit. It's delicious.
   _____

2. I don't like vegetables at all.
   _____

3. Do you like coffee?
   _____

4. Would you like some coffee?
   _____

5. I'd like some water, please.
   _____

6. Is there any bread?
   _____

7. Yes, there is some, but there isn't much.
   _____

8. Are there any cookies?
   _____

9. Yes, there are some, but there aren't many.
   _____

10. Could you pass the salt, please?
    _____

# 10 Looking good!

**Grammar:** Present Continuous • Spelling of verb + -ing • Whose is it?
**Vocabulary:** Parts of the body • In a clothing store

## Present Continuous

### 1 I'm working hard because . . .
Match a line in **A** with a line in **B**.

| A | B |
|---|---|
| 1. I'm studying hard | a. because he doesn't earn much. |
| 2. Len's buying his wife a present | b. because they're dry and the sun's hot. |
| 3. Diana's washing her hair | c. because it's her birthday soon. |
| 4. Jin's looking for a better job | d. because I have exams next week. |
| 5. We're buying some new clothes | e. because he's hungry. |
| 6. She's watering the flowers | f. because she's going to a party tonight. |
| 7. The baby's crying | g. because we're going to a wedding soon. |

### 2 Spelling of verb + -ing
Write the -ing form of the verbs.

1. walk  __walking__
2. have  _____
3. read  _____
4. stop  _____
5. use  _____
6. listen  _____
7. run  _____
8. say  _____

9. swim  _____
10. come  _____
11. do  _____
12. put  _____
13. ride  _____
14. drive  _____
15. think  _____

### 3 What are you doing?
Write sentences that are true for you.

1. wearing a suit  __I'm not wearing a suit.__
2. wearing sneakers  _____
3. listening to the teacher  _____
4. sitting in my bedroom  _____
5. working with a friend  _____
6. doing an English exercise  _____
7. drinking coffee  _____
8. my parents working  _____

### 4 Making questions
Put the words in the correct order to make questions in the Present Continuous.

1. you / what / are / doing / ?
   __What are you doing?__

2. cooking / are / you / what / ?
   _____
   _____

3. tonight / out / you / going / are / ?
   _____
   _____

4. playing / we / time / tennis / what / are / ?
   _____
   _____

5. crying / daughter / why / is / your / ?
   _____
   _____

6. dinner / are / and / Renata / Fernando / for / coming / when / ?
   _____
   _____

## 5 Describing people

1 Look at the people in the pictures. Describe them. What are they wearing? What are they doing? Write some sentences about them.

Alice

George

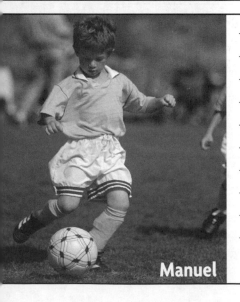
Manuel

2 **CD 40** Correct the descriptions of the people.

**Alice**
1. ☑ Alice's wearing a dress.
2. ☒ She has long blonde hair.   *She has short grey hair.*
3. ☐ She's reading a book in her bedroom.

**George**
4. ☐ George is wearing a dark suit and tie.
5. ☐ He has short grey hair and he's wearing glasses.
6. ☐ He's cooking in the kitchen.

**Manuel**
7. ☐ Manuel's wearing shorts and a T-shirt.
8. ☐ He has short blonde hair.
9. ☐ He's playing soccer in the yard.

# Present Continuous and Simple

6 **What do they do? What are they doing?**

Look at the pictures and answer the questions.

1. What does Tom do?            *He's a pilot.*
2. Is he flying a plane now?     *No, he isn't.*
3. What's he doing?             _____
4. What does Fiona do?          _____
5. Is she designing buildings now? _____
6. What's she doing?            _____
7. What does Brian do?          _____
8. Is he delivering letters now? _____
9. What does Jess do?           _____
10. Is she working in a store now? _____
11. What's she doing?           _____

Brian

I'm a mail carrier.

## 7 Present Continuous or Present Simple?

1 Choose the correct form of the verb.

1. *I take / I'm taking* a shower every morning.
2. Look! *It's raining. / It rains.* We can't go to the beach.
3. What *are you doing / do you do* tonight? *Are you going / Do you go* out?
4. What *are we having / do we have* for dinner tonight?
5. Where *are you usually going / do you usually go* on vacation?
6. What *are you doing / do you do* under the table?
7. *I'm trying / I try* to find my pen.

Tom

I'm a pilot.

I'm a sales assistant.

Jess

Fiona

I'm an architect.

2 Complete the sentences with the verb in the Present Continuous or Present Simple.

1. **rain**
   Oh, no! It <u>'s raining</u>. We can't play tennis.
   It always _____ a lot in April.

2. **read**
   I _____ a very good book right now.
   I _____ in bed every night.

3. **drink**
   I'm _____ a big bottle of water because it's very hot today.
   I always _____ a lot of water on hot days.

4. **work**
   She's a doctor. She _____ in St. Mary's Hospital.
   She _____ hard because she has an exam tomorrow.

5. **not eat**
   I _____ that! It looks disgusting!
   Vegetarians _____ meat.

6. **speak**
   Look! Pat _____ Korean to that man over there.
   How many languages _____ he _____?

7. **do**
   Why _____ we _____ exercises?
   Why _____ we _____ this exercise now?

## 8 Auxiliary verbs

Complete the sentences with *am/is/are* or *do/does/don't/doesn't*.

1. John's a vegetarian. He _____ eat meat.
2. **A** Where _____ you going?
   **B** I _____ going to the bank.
3. How many children _____ your sister have?
4. **A** I _____ looking for a pair of black shoes.
   **B** Certainly. What size _____ you take?
5. **A** Why _____ Daniel studying Chinese?
   **B** Because he _____ going to China on vacation.
6. **A** Hola! ¿Qué tal?
   **B** Sorry. I _____ understand. I _____ speak Spanish.
7. **A** What _____ you want to do tonight?
   **B** Why _____ we go and see James?
   **A** We can't, because he _____ working late tonight.

# Whose is this? It's his

## 9 Whose book is this?

Look at the people in the pictures. Write questions and answers about the objects.

1. book? **Whose book is this? It's hers.** _____
2. bikes? _____
3. hat? _____
4. car? _____
5. sunglasses? _____
6. sneakers? _____
7. suntan lotion? _____
8. sports bag? _____
9. dog? _____
10. ball? _____

## 10 It's ours

CD 41 Rewrite the sentences with the possessive pronoun.

1. It's our school.      **It's ours.** _____
2. It's my book. _____
3. It's your idea. _____
4. They're their tickets. _____
5. They're her jeans. _____
6. This is my car. _____
7. This is your briefcase. _____
8. These are your pens. _____

## 11 Is it correct?

Correct the sentences.

1. Where your sister work?
   **Where does your sister work?** _____

2. I'm go to the movies tonight.
   _____

3. Who's jacket is this on your chair?
   _____

4. We no wear a uniform at my school.
   _____

5. That's my husband over there. He stands near the window.
   _____
   _____

6. What you doing after school today?
   _____

7. Sorry. You can't speak to Jenny. She's take a shower.
   _____
   _____

8. Whose that girl over there? She looks nice.
   _____

9. Peter's a businessman. He's work all over the world.
   _____
   _____

10. Right now Peter's work in Tokyo.
    _____

# Vocabulary

## 12 Parts of the body

1 Label the picture using the words in the box.

| eyes | leg | arm | ~~head~~ | feet | hand | face | hair |
|------|-----|-----|----------|------|------|------|------|

1. <u>head</u>          4. _____     7. _____
2. _____     5. _____     8. _____
3. _____     6. _____

2 Now describe each person.

The woman <u>is tall. She has short dark hair. She's wearing ...</u>
_____
_____
_____

The man _____
_____
_____
_____

# Check it

## 13 Listening – In a clothing store

**CD 42** Listen and answer the questions.

1. What is the woman looking for?
   _____

2. Which one does she try on?
   _____

3. What's wrong with it?
   _____

4. What does the sales assistant do?
   _____

5. What does she buy?
   _____

6. How does she pay?
   _____
   _____

## 14 Translation

Translate these sentences.

1. He is very handsome.
   _____

2. She is smiling.
   _____

3. Adriana is speaking to Mayumi.
   _____

4. Adriana speaks three languages.
   _____

5. Whose baby is this? He's theirs.
   _____

6. Whose boots are these? They're his.
   _____

7. We're having a party on Saturday.
   _____

8. Can I try this shirt on?
   _____

9. I like this one much better.
   _____

10. I'll take it.
    _____

# 11 Life's an adventure!

## going to

### 1 What are they going to be?

Read about the people. Write sentences using the words in the box.

| pilot | journalist | architect | interpreter |
|-------|-----------|-----------|-------------|
| pianist | teacher | doctor | athlete |

1. **Francisco and I** are learning to fly.
   **We're going to be pilots.**

2. **Bob** loves children.

3. **Maria**'s good at languages.

4. **Ming** likes writing.

5. **Sue and Peter** are studying medicine.

6. **Jane** likes modern buildings.

7. **Kwan**'s good at playing the piano.

8. **Emilia** can run very fast.

### 2 What is going to happen?

Complete the sentences with *going to* and a verb or phrase from the box.

| jump | snow | be sick | be late |
|------|------|---------|---------|
| drive | leave | have a job interview | |

1. Look at that boy on the wall! I think
   he **'s going to jump**.

2. I don't feel well. I think I_____.

3. It's so cold and look at those clouds! I think
   it_____.

4. This movie's so boring. We_____.

5. Amelia's wearing her best clothes.
   She_____.

6. Hurry up! It's nearly ten o'clock!
   You_____.

7. **A** Do you want to walk to the stores?
   **B** No, I_____.

### 3 Making questions

**CD 43** Write the questions for these sentences.

1. I'm very hungry.
   (What / you / eat?)
   **What are you going to eat?**

2. We're going to the movies.
   (What / you / see?)

3. Yukio's coming for dinner tonight.
   (What / you / cook?)

4. Cathy's going to college in September.
   (What / she / study?)

5. Tim and Jill got engaged last week.
   (When / they / get married?)

6. Hong's not going by train.
   (he / fly?)

7. It's my birthday next week.
   (you / have a party?)

8. It's very cloudy.
   (it / rain?)

## 4 Going on vacation

1 **CD 44** Listen and complete the information about Laura and Mike's vacation.

2 Make notes about your next vacation.

| | Laura and Mike | James | Me |
|---|---|---|---|
| **Where?** | Puerto Rico | Montreal | |
| **How/travel?** | | train | |
| **Where/stay?** | | the Hotel du Fort | |
| **How long/stay?** | | 6 days | |
| **What/do?** | | visit Old Montreal | |

3 Write sentences about Laura and Mike's plans.

1. **Laura and Mike are going to Puerto Rico.**
2. They _____
3. _____
4. _____
5. _____

4 Complete the conversation between Laura and James.

**Laura** (1) _____ on vacation next summer?

**James** To Montreal.

**Laura** (2) _____ fly there?

**James** No, I'm not. I'm going by train.

**Laura** (3) _____?

**James** In a hotel. The Hotel du Fort.

**Laura** (4) _____?

**James** For six days, from Friday to Wednesday.

**Laura** And (5) _____?

**James** Well, (6) _____, because the buildings are really beautiful.

5 Write five sentences about your next vacation.

1. _____
2. _____
3. _____
4. _____
5. _____

## 5 Making negatives

Read the sentences about the past. Make negative sentences about the future.

1. Sue and Bill got a new car last year.
   **They aren't going to get one this year.**

2. James had a birthday party last year.
   _____

3. We went to Venezuela last year.
   _____

4. I wore my blue coat yesterday.
   _____

5. Pedro and Julia did the dishes yesterday.
   _____

6. My aunt gave me a hat for my birthday last year.
   _____

7. Kato didn't pass the exam last year.

# Comparatives

## 6 Forming comparative adjectives

1 **CD 45** Write the adjectives.

| Adjective | Comparative |
|---|---|
| 1. *cheap* | cheaper |
| 2. *dirty* | dirtier |
| 3. _____ | faster |
| 4. _____ | safer |
| 5. _____ | friendlier |
| 6. _____ | bigger |
| 7. _____ | noisier |
| 8. _____ | hotter |
| 9. _____ | more exciting |
| 10. _____ | more modern |

2 Write the opposites of the comparative adjectives.

| Comparative | Opposite |
|---|---|
| 1. faster | *slower* |
| 2. safer | *more dangerous* |
| 3. bigger | _____ |
| 4. cheaper | _____ |
| 5. cleaner | _____ |
| 6. more boring | _____ |
| 7. more difficult | _____ |
| 8. colder | _____ |
| 9. further | _____ |
| 10. better | _____ |

## 7 more . . . /-er than

Complete the sentences using the comparative form of the adjective.

1. The town isn't very clean. The country <u>is cleaner than</u> the town.
2. My car isn't very new. Your car _____ my car.
3. Ann's house isn't very modern. Your house _____ Ann's.
4. Bob's backyard isn't very big. Your backyard _____ much _____ Bob's.
5. Yesterday wasn't very hot. Today _____ much _____ yesterday.
6. Sue's homework wasn't very good. Your homework _____ _____ Sue's.
7. Your car isn't very dirty. My car _____ yours.
8. This exercise isn't very difficult. The next exercise _____ much _____ this one!

# Comparatives and superlatives

## 8 Comparative and superlative adjectives

**CD 46** Write the comparative and superlative forms of the adjectives.

| Adjective | Comparative | Superlative |
|---|---|---|
| 1. cheap | *cheaper* | *the cheapest* |
| 2. expensive | *more expensive* | *the most expensive* |
| 3. young | _____ | _____ |
| 4. happy | _____ | _____ |
| 5. beautiful | _____ | _____ |
| 6. big | _____ | _____ |
| 7. busy | _____ | _____ |
| 8. intelligent | _____ | _____ |
| 9. bad | _____ | _____ |
| 10. far | _____ | _____ |
| 11. new | _____ | _____ |
| 12. dangerous | _____ | _____ |

## 9 Word order

Put the words in the correct order to make sentences or questions.

1. family / the / am / my / in / I / oldest
   **I am the oldest in my family.**

2. sister / me / my / than / younger / is

   _____

3. class / who / oldest / the / the / in / is / ?

   _____

4. passenger / plane / was / Concorde / world / fastest / the / in / the

   _____

5. book / interesting / than / my / your / more / is / book

   _____

6. bought / expensive / store / the / in / watch / most / Peter / the

   _____

7. cheapest / buy / you / store / in / the / the / did / watch / ?

   _____

8. difficult / German / English / is / than / more / much

   _____

9. weather / better / today / than / much / was / yesterday / the

   _____

# Auxiliary verbs

## 10 am/is/are, do/does/did

Complete the sentences with *am/is/are* or *do/does/did*.

1. _____ he play tennis last Sunday?
2. _____ he playing tennis now?
3. How often _____ you wash your hair?
4. _____ you wash it yesterday?
5. I _____ going to wash it tonight.
6. We _____ having dinner at the moment.
7. _____ you have dinner at this time every night?
8. What _____ your parents going to do when they retire?
9. When _____ your parents first meet?
10. What time _____ Marina usually arrive at school?

## 11 Short answers

**CD 47** Write true answers.

1. Are you a student? **Yes, I am.**
2. Are you going to Australia next year?

   _____

3. Do you have a sister?

   _____

4. Did you watch TV last night?

   _____

5. Do you live in a city?

   _____

6. Does your teacher talk a lot?

   _____

7. Is your teacher talking at the moment?

   _____

8. Did your teacher give you some homework yesterday?

   _____

9. Is your teacher going to give you some homework today?

   _____

10. Does your teacher have long hair?

    _____

11. Can you speak Japanese?

    _____

# Vocabulary and pronunciation

## 12 Word stress

**CD 48** Look at these words from Units 1–11. How many syllables do they have? Where is the stress? Put them into the correct columns.

| | | | |
|---|---|---|---|
| ~~mountain~~ | ~~guitar~~ | ~~tomorrow~~ | ~~yesterday~~ |
| important | suitcase | machine | hospital |
| piano | hotel | dangerous | dessert |
| delicious | languages | along | beautiful |
| homework | umbrella | boyfriend | airport |

| A | B | C | D |
|---|---|---|---|
| • • | • • | • • • | • • • |
| mountain | guitar | tomorrow | yesterday |
| _____ | _____ | _____ | _____ |
| _____ | _____ | _____ | _____ |
| _____ | _____ | _____ | _____ |
| _____ | _____ | _____ | _____ |

## 13 Phonetic spelling

The words in phonetic spelling have two syllables. Write the words and mark the correct stress.

                           • •

1. /'trævl/    travel _____
2. /'weðə/    _____
3. /fər'get/    _____
4. /'fri:dəm/    _____
5. /'speʃəl/    _____
6. /'lɪsən/    _____
7. /'i:vnɪŋ/    _____
8. /rɪ'læks/    _____

## 14 Matching sounds

Which words rhyme with the letters?

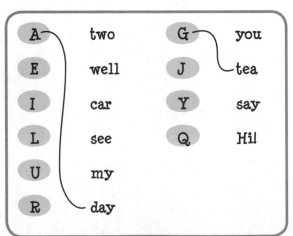

| | | | |
|---|---|---|---|
| A | two | G | you |
| E | well | J | tea |
| I | car | Y | say |
| L | see | Q | Hi! |
| U | my | | |
| R | day | | |

# Prepositions

## 15 *from, like, than . . .*

Complete the sentences with a preposition from the box.

| from | like | than | in | at | for | of | on |

1. Look _____ that picture. Isn't it beautiful?
2. What do we have _____ dinner? I'm hungry.
3. Our hotel is fifty meters _____ the sea.
4. What is the longest river _____ the world?
5. Canada is much bigger _____ the United States.
6. I'm looking _____ Chris. Where is he?
7. Can you buy a bottle _____ milk at the store?
8. Mariela is _____ her sister in many ways. They're both beautiful and intelligent.
9. Come and see me _____ seven o'clock.
10. What did you do _____ the weekend?
11. _____ Saturday night we went to a party.
12. We went shopping _____ the morning.

# Check it

## 16 Translation

Translate the sentences.

1. I'm going to leave tomorrow.

   _____

2. I'm not going to retire until I'm 70.

   _____

3. I'm leaving tomorrow.

   _____

4. I'm going to Hawaii next week.

   _____

5. I went home early.

   _____

6. What's the weather like today?

   _____

7. What should we do today?

   _____

8. Should we go swimming?

   _____

9. Let's go swimming!

   _____

10. I'll get my swimsuit.

    _____

## 17 Listening – Making suggestions

**CD 49** Laura and Mike are on vacation in Puerto Rico. Listen and check (✓) the things they decide to do today.

- [ ] go to the beach
- [ ] go sailing
- [ ] go swimming
- [ ] go into town
- [ ] go by taxi
- [ ] catch a bus
- [ ] look at the town center
- [ ] go to the tourist office
- [ ] look at the stores
- [ ] buy some postcards
- [ ] buy sun hats
- [ ] buy some souvenirs
- [ ] have lunch in a restaurant
- [ ] practice speaking Spanish

# 12 Have you ever?

**Grammar:** Present Perfect • Time expressions
**Vocabulary:** *been* or *gone*? • Compound nouns • Saying good-bye

## Present Perfect

### 1 Verb forms

Write the Past Simple and the past participle forms of the verbs. Two verbs are regular.

| Infinitive | Past Simple | Past participle |
|---|---|---|
| come | came | come |
| arrive | arrived | arrived |
| leave | | |
| write | | |
| speak | | |
| see | | |
| have | | |
| do | | |
| meet | | |
| take | | |
| ride | | |
| give | | |
| finish | | |
| fly | | |
| buy | | |

### 2 Present Perfect or Past Simple?

1 Read about Maria Sharapova and choose the correct form of the verb.

2 **CD 50** Write short answers to the questions about Maria Sharapova.

1. Has Maria won the Wimbledon tennis tournament?
   __Yes, she has.__

2. Did she go to the United States five years ago?
   __No, she didn't.__

3. Did she start playing tennis when she was three?
   _____

4. Have Maria and her father traveled a lot?
   _____

5. Have they ever been to France?
   _____

6. Did they go to France in May?
   _____

7. Did she win the tournament?
   _____

8. Has she won the U.S. Open yet?
   _____

# Maria Sharapova

**Tennis player**

Maria Sharapova is a tennis player. She is only 17 years old, but she (1) *already won/has already won* the Wimbledon Women's tennis tournament! She (2) *started/has started* playing tennis with her father when she was four years old. Three years later she (3) *went/has gone* to the U.S. to Nic Bollettieri's famous Tennis Academy in Florida.

Maria and her father (4) *traveled/have traveled* to many countries. In May they (5) *went/have gone* to the French Open. Maria (6) *played/has played* well, but she (7) *didn't win/hasn't won*. She (8) *didn't win/hasn't won* any other major tournaments yet, but she plans to win another one soon!

56   Unit 12 · Have you ever?

**3** Complete the story. Put the verb in parentheses into the Present Perfect or Past Simple tense.

## A sad story of a sad man

One Sunday evening two men (1) _____ (meet) in a Los Angeles cafe. One of them was very unhappy.

"Life is terrible, everything in the world is really boring," he said.

"Don't say that," said the other man. "Life is wonderful! The world is so exciting! Think about Italy. It's a wonderful country. (2) _____ you ever _____ (be) there?"

"Oh, yes. I (3) _____ (go) there last year and I (4) _____ (not like) it."

"Well, (5) _____ you _____ (be) to China? (6) _____ you ever _____ (see) the Great Wall?"

"Oh, yes. I (7) _____ (go) there for my honeymoon and we (8) _____ (see) the Great Wall of China. I (9) _____ (not enjoy) it."

"Well, I just (10) _____ (return) from a safari in Africa. (11) _____ you _____ (visit) Africa yet?"

"Yes, I (12) _____ (go) on safari in East Africa last year and I (13) _____ (climb) Mount Kilimanjaro. It was really boring."

"Well," said the other man, "I think that you're very ill. Only the best psychiatrist in Los Angeles can help you. Go to see Dr. Greenbaum on Harley Street."

"But I am Dr. Greenbaum," answered the man sadly.

## Time expressions

### 3 *ever* and *never*

**1** Read the answers about Tara, Ryan's fiancée from the U.S. Use the words to write questions with *ever*.

1. Barcelona?
   **Have you ever been to Barcelona?**
   *No, never.*

2. travel by train?
   **Have you ever traveled by train?**
   *Yes, I have, four times.*

3. Rome?
   _____?
   *No, never.*

4. fly to Mexico?
   _____?
   *Yes, I have, twice.*

5. New York?
   _____?
   *Yes, I have, many of times. My fiancé Ryan lives there.*

6. ride on a tour bus?
   _____?
   *Yes, I have, in New York!*

7. visited Taiwan?
   _____?
   *No, I haven't. But I want to!*

**2** Use the information to write sentences about Tara.

1. **Tara hasn't been to Barcelona.**
2. **She's traveled by train four times.**
3. _____
4. _____
5. _____
6. _____
7. _____

## 4  *ago* and *last week*

Write sentences in the Past Simple using a pronoun and the time expressions in parentheses.

1. I've seen the latest Bond movie. (last week)
   **I saw it last week.**

2. The taxi has arrived. (five minutes ago)
   It _____

3. We've seen the Taj Majal. (in 1997)
   _____

4. She's written the letter. (yesterday)
   _____

5. I've done my homework. (after dinner)
   _____

6. They've had lunch. (at twelve o'clock)
   _____

## 5  *yet*

**CD 51** Rewrite the sentences with *yet*. Use a pronoun if possible.

1. Sarah and Tom are going to have lunch.
   **They haven't had lunch yet.**

2. Mary's going to wash her hair.
   _____

3. Mr. and Mrs. Gibbs are going to visit their son.
   _____

4. Juan's going to take a shower.
   _____

5. Bill and I are going to move to a house next week.
   _____

6. My aunt is going to give me a birthday present.
   _____

## 6  Choosing the correct adverb

Choose one of the adverbs in parentheses and put it in the correct place in the sentence. Only one adverb in each pair is correct.

1. I saw Joel ten days. (ago / ever)
   **I saw Joel ten days ago.**

2. Have you tried Japanese food? (last year / ever)
   _____

3. Have you finished writing your book? (yet / ever)
   _____

4. I've seen anyone who eats more than you. (ever / never)
   _____

5. Are there any letters for me? I saw the mail carrier.
   (ago / just) _____

6. We went out to a restaurant. (ever / yesterday)
   _____

## 7  *yet* and *just*

Use the words to write questions with *yet*, then write answers with *just*.

1. you / clean your room?
   A **Have you cleaned your room yet?**
   B **Yes, I just cleaned it.**

2. Ann / speak to the bank manager?
   A _____?
   B  Yes, _____ to him.

3. Mark / make a cup of coffee?
   A _____?
   B  Yes, _____ one.

4. do / your homework?
   A _____?
   B  Yes, _____ it.

5. Mr. Jones / read the report?
   A _____?
   B  Yes, _____ it.

6. you / call a taxi?
   A _____?
   B  Yes, _____ one.

# Check it

## 8  Translation

Translate these sentences.

1. I've been to France.
   _____

2. I went there two years ago.
   _____

3. I haven't been to Australia.
   _____

4. I haven't been to Australia yet.
   _____

5. Have you seen Tara?
   _____

6. I just saw her. She was in the clothing store.
   _____

7. It's been a wonderful vacation. I can't believe it's over.
   _____

8. Well, you haven't missed anything here. Nothing much has happened!
   _____

# *been* or *gone*?

## 9 *she's been/she's gone*

1 Look at the pictures. What is the difference between *been* and *gone*?

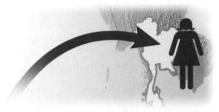

She's gone to Thailand.

She's been to Thailand.

- *She's gone to Thailand.*
  = She's in Thailand now.
- *She's been to Thailand.*
  = She went to Thailand and now she has returned.

2 Complete the sentences with *been* or *gone*.

1. Ichiro's not here. He's _____ to work.

2. The office is empty. Everybody has _____ home.

3. It's good to see you again. Where have you _____?

4. My brother's _____ to the U.S. four times.

5. Sorry, you can't speak to Kanya. She's _____ to a party.

6. Ann is back in the office today. She's _____ on vacation since Monday.

7. Daniel's _____ to Canada and he's staying there for three weeks.

# Vocabulary

## 10 Compound nouns

1 Look at these examples of compound nouns.

ticket + office = ticket office
mail + box = mailbox

Match a noun in **A** with a noun in **B** to make a new noun.

| A | B |
|---|---|
| 1. town | a. lot |
| 2. train | b. agent |
| 3. traffic | c. center |
| 4. cell | d. office |
| 5. parking | e. station |
| 6. travel | f. port |
| 7. post | g. phone |
| 8. air | h. lights |

2 Complete the sentences with the correct compound noun.

1. Can I borrow your _____ to call my mom?

2. I'm late for my train! Could you drive me to the _____?

3. Chicago's O'Hare is one of the biggest _____ in the world.

4. We took the bus to the _____ to meet our friends in the cafe.

5. Lisa Jones is a great _____. She found a cheap ticket for me.

## 11 Listening – Saying good-bye

**CD 52** Listen to So-young's conversation at the airport. Correct the incorrect sentences.

1. ✗ So-young is checking in her luggage.
   *So-young has checked in her luggage.*

2. ☐ So-young has a window seat.
   _____

3. ☐ So-young has lost her ticket.
   _____

4. ☐ Becky is visiting So-young next spring.
   _____

5. ☐ Flight 172 is boarding at gate 13.
   _____

6. ☐ So-young is flying to Seoul.
   _____

# Review

## Verb *to be*

### 1  Questions

Match a question in **A** with an answer in **B**.

| A | B |
|---|---|
| 1. Where's Machu Picchu? | a. No, I'm not. |
| 2. What's your name? | b. He's 33. |
| 3. How old is Jeff? | c. No, she isn't. |
| 4. Where are they from? | d. 50 cents. |
| 5. How are the children? | e. It's in Peru. |
| 6. What's your job? | f. Mexico. |
| 7. Are they married? | g. They're fine. |
| 8. How much is an orange? | h. I'm a doctor. |
| 9. Is she Korean? | i. Yes, they are. |
| 10. Are you in college? | j. I'm Sue. |

### 2  Making negatives

Correct the sentences.

1. Rome is in Spain.

   **Rome isn't in Spain. It's in Italy.**

2. Bananas are blue.

3. Tokyo is the capital of China.

4. You're from Canada.

5. The day after Thursday is Wednesday.

6. Chicago is in Canada.

7. New York and São Paulo are small cities.

### 3  Making questions

Put the words in the correct order to make questions.

1. married / she / is / ?

   **Is she married?**

2. children / old / are / how / your / ?

3. number / her / what / phone / is / ?

4. the / apartment / city / in / is / your / ?

5. brother / home / your / is / at / ?

6. the / much / sandwiches / how / are / chicken / ?

7. name / is / your / what / first / ?

### 4  Short forms

Write the short forms.

1. It is hot today.

   **It's hot today.**

2. My brother is not married.

3. I am not a student.

4. Where is the university?

5. You are twenty-nine.

6. We are at school.

7. She is cold and I am hot.

# Present Simple

## 1 Present Simple affirmative

Complete the sentence with a suitable verb.

1. She _____plays_____ tennis every day.
2. My daughter _____ French and Portuguese.
3. Jed's a pilot. He _____ all over the world.
4. Actors _____ in hotels a lot.
5. Stephanie _____ to work by bus.
6. He _____ television every evening.
7. I _____ from Monterrey.

## 2 Present Simple negative

Write negative sentences.

1. I / not like skiing. **I don't like skiing.**
2. They / not live / Boston.

   _____

3. He / not write letters every day.

   _____

4. We / not have / car.

   _____

5. Eric and Lina / not like getting up.

   _____

6. Rachel / not eat meat.

   _____

7. It / not cost 50¢.

   _____

## 3 Present Simple questions

Write questions for these answers.

1. **Where does he work?**   He works in a bank.
2. _____?

   They get up at 6:30.
3. _____?

   She speaks Spanish and Portuguese.
4. _____?

   I live in Seattle.
5. _____?

   We finish school at 4:00.
6. _____?

   I work in an office.
7. _____?

   She has coffee and toast.

## 4 Daily routines

1 Complete the information about your daily routine.

|  | Tom | you |
|---|---|---|
| get up<br>breakfast<br>go to work/school | 8:00<br>coffee/orange juice<br>by car | |
| lunch<br>finish work/school | in a restaurant<br>5:30 | |
| dinner<br>in the evening<br>go to bed | 7:15<br>listen to music<br>11:30 | |

2 Write sentences.

1. **Tom gets up at 8:00. I get up at 7:30.**
2. _____
3. _____
4. _____
5. _____
6. _____
7. _____
8. _____

## 5 What does she do?

Complete the text with the correct form of the verbs from the box.

| be | not eat | go | live | study | work |
|---|---|---|---|---|---|
| get up | not finish | love | not like | finish | fly |
| start | have | eat | visit | stay | want |

**Philippa Robbins** (1) _____is_____ a scientist. She (2) _____ in an apartment in Princeton, New Jersey, and she (3) _____ biology at the university. Every day she (4) _____ at 6:30 and (5) _____ three cups of coffee. She (6) _____ anything for breakfast. She (7) _____ work in her laboratory at 7:00, and she (8) _____ until lunchtime. Then she (9) _____ for a short walk in the park. She usually (10) _____ work at 6:00, but sometimes she (11) _____ until 10:00. In the evening she often (12) _____ in a restaurant because she (13) _____ cooking. Every winter she and her husband (14) _____ to Florida, where they (15) _____ a laboratory. They (16) _____ in a friend's house for two weeks. They never (17) _____ to go back to Princeton because they (18) _____ hot weather!

## 6 do, does, is, or are?

Complete the sentences with a verb from the box.

| do | don't | does | doesn't |
|----|-------|------|---------|
| is | isn't | are | aren't |

1. He's a vegetarian—he __doesn't__ eat meat.
2. She _____ want a pizza—she _____ hungry.
3. _____ the museum close at 5:00?
4. _____ you know how much a cup of coffee _____ ?
5. I _____ know where they _____ from, but they _____ American.
6. We _____ want to go to Mexico, but they _____ .
7. I _____ think the bank _____ open today.
8. _____ Stephanie know where the meeting _____ ?
9. Where _____ Chris and Mike? They _____ usually late for work.

## there is / are

### 1 Describing a room

Answer the questions about the room you are in now.

1. Is there a telephone?        __No, there isn't.__
2. Are there any windows?        _____
3. How many chairs are there?        _____
4. Is there a television?        _____
5. Are there any pictures?        _____
6. How many books are there?        _____
7. How many lamps are there?        _____

## 2 Describing a hotel

Barbara and David want to go to a hotel in North Carolina on vacation. Read the advertisement, then complete the telephone conversation between Barbara and the hotel receptionist.

**SMOKY MOUNTAINS COUNTRY LODGE HOTEL**

Come and experience real hospitality in this beautiful hotel in the mountains of North Carolina. Good walks in the countryside.

For information and reservations call (828) 317-5111

**R** Hello, the Smoky Mountains Country Lodge Hotel.

**B** Oh, hello. Can you tell me something about the hotel please? How many rooms are there?

**R** (1) _____ twenty, all with private bathrooms.

**B** Oh, that's good. (2) _____ televisions in the rooms?

**R** No, (3) _____ . But (4) _____ a television room.

**B** And (5) _____ any sports facilities?

**R** Yes, (6) _____ two tennis courts.

**B** (7) _____ a swimming pool?

**R** No, (8) _____ .

**B** And (9) _____ a restaurant in the hotel?

**R** Yes, (10) _____ . The food is excellent, and (11) _____ an open fire.

**B** Great! And (12) _____ a town near the hotel?

**R** Yes, Waynesville is five miles away. (13) _____ cafes and stores there, too.

# can/can't

## 1  Affirmative and negative

What can Penny and Keith do? Complete the sentences.

|  | Penny | Keith |
|---|---|---|
| play the guitar | ✗ | ✗ |
| cook | ✓ | ✓ |
| swim | ✗ | ✓ |
| do crosswords | ✓ | ✗ |
| draw | ✓ | ✗ |

1. Penny ____can't____ play the guitar.
2. Keith _____ draw, but Penny _____ .
3. Keith can _____ , but Penny _____ .
4. Penny and Keith can _____ .
5. Penny _____ do crosswords, but Keith

    _____ .

## 2  Questions

Complete the questions with *can* and a suitable verb.
Then answer the questions.

1. ____Can____ you ____ride____ a motorcycle?

   __Yes, I can.__

2. _____ you _____ a musical

   instrument?

   _____

3. _____ you _____ Chinese?

   _____

4. _____ you _____ a car?

   _____

5. _____ you _____ a computer?

   _____

6. _____ you _____ chess?

   _____

7. _____ you _____ a bicycle?

   _____

# Past Simple

## 1  Regular and irregular verbs

Complete the sentences. Put the verbs in parentheses
into the Past Simple.

1. I ___started___ (start) school when I was four.
2. I _____ (work) until 8:00, and then I

   _____ (meet) some friends and we

   _____ (go) to the movies.
3. She _____ (sell) her old car and

   _____ (buy) a new one.
4. I _____ (play) tennis in the morning, but it

   _____ (rain) in the afternoon, so I

   _____ (study) for my exams.
5. Last week we _____ (drive) to Dallas

   and _____ (visit) our grandparents.
6. I _____ (lose) my umbrella last week—I

   _____ (leave) it in the bank and someone

   _____ (steal) it.
7. He _____ (retire) and _____ (move)

   to the country.

## 2  Past Simple negative

Make the verbs negative.

1. He went to Thailand.

   __He didn't go to Thailand.__

2. They won a vacation in the Caribbean.

   _____

3. We were at home yesterday.

   _____

4. Dickens wrote sixteen novels.

   _____

5. Columbus was born in Genoa.

   _____

6. She spent a week in the Alps.

   _____

7. I brought you a present.

   _____

## 3 Past Simple questions

Put the words in the correct order to make questions. Then write true answers.

1. you / high school / when / graduate / did / from

   <u>When did you leave school</u> _____?

   <u>I left school when I was eighteen.</u> _____

2. you / were / where / born

   _____?

   _____

3. morning / at / you / were / 10:00 / yesterday / where

   _____?

   _____

4. time / bed / did / to / last / go / night / what / you

   _____?

   _____

5. in / when / you / country / last / did / walk / the

   _____?

   _____

6. many / month / did / last / see / movies / you / how

   _____?

   _____

7. last / a / restaurant / week / did / eat / you / in

   _____?

   _____

## 4 Describing a vacation

Read the information and complete the conversation about Julian and Nicole's last vacation.

| Where / go? | Brazil |
|---|---|
| How long / spend there? | two weeks |
| When / come back? | Friday |
| How / travel? | plane and car |
| Where / stay? | not much money, cheap hotels |
| What / do? | the north—walked, ate a lot, photographs |
| | Rio de Janeiro, not much time |
| Enjoy the beach? | Yes |
| What / bring back? | coffee |

**Helen** Where ___*did*___ you and Nicole ___*go*___ for your last vacation?

**Julian** We (1) _____ to Brazil.

**Helen** Oh, how nice! How long (2) _____ you _____ there?

**Julian** Only two weeks. We (3) _____ last Friday.

**Helen** And how (4) _____ you _____?

**Julian** We (5) _____ to Rio de Janeiro, and then we (6) _____ around the country.

**Helen** And where (7) _____ you _____?

**Julian** Well, we (8) _____ much money, so we (9) _____ in cheap hotels.

**Helen** And what (10) _____ you _____?

**Julian** In the north we (11) _____ walking, (12) _____ Brazilian coffee, and (13) _____ lots of food! And Nicole (14) _____ hundreds of photos. In Rio we (15) _____ to some great beaches, but we (16) _____ time to see everything.

**Helen** (17) _____ you _____ the vacation?

**Julian** Yes, it (18) _____ fantastic.

**Helen** And (19) _____ you _____ anything back?

**Julian** Yes, we (20) _____ a lot of coffee—here's some for you!

# like

## 1 What do you like doing?

Make sentences about what you like doing.

1. go / dentist
   **I don't like going to the dentist.**

2. play / computer games
   _____

3. buy / clothes
   _____

4. listen / music
   _____

5. swim / the ocean
   _____

6. study / English
   _____

7. sleep / tent
   _____

## 2 *like* and *would like*

Choose the correct sentence. Put ✓ and ✗.

1. **A** Would you like a banana?
   **B** ✗ Yes, I do.
   **B** ✓ Yes, please.

2. ☐ I'm hungry. I like a sandwich.
   ☐ I'm hungry. I'd like a sandwich.

3. **A** Do you like reading?
   **B** ☐ Yes, I do.
   **B** ☐ Yes, I like.

4. ☐ Do you like a drink?
   ☐ Would you like a drink?

5. ☐ I like red cars.
   ☐ I'd like red cars.

6. **A** Can I help you?
   **B** ☐ I'd like a ticket, please.
   **B** ☐ I like a ticket, please.

7. **A** Would you like an apple?
   **B** ☐ No, thanks.
   **B** ☐ No, I don't.

8. ☐ She likes go to the movies.
   ☐ She likes going to the movies.

9. **A** Do you like oranges?
   **B** ☐ Yes, I'd like.
   **B** ☐ Yes, I do.

# Present Continuous

## 1 Present Continuous affirmative and negative

Complete the sentences with the Present Continuous form of the verb in parentheses.

1. We can't go climbing. **It's raining**____. (rain)
2. Why _____ you _____ for your keys? (look)
3. Oh no! The DVD _____. (not work)
4. How _____ she _____? (feel)
5. We _____ today, we're tired. (not swim)
6. What _____ you _____ at? (laugh)
7. OK, wait a minute, I _____ now. (get up)
8. I _____ dinner for twelve people! (not cook)

## 2 Present Continuous questions

Put the words in the correct order to make questions.

1. you / are / on / going / vacation / where **Where are you going on vacation**?
2. they / dancing / tonight / are / going
   _____?
3. she / driving / train / is / by / or / going
   _____?
4. buying / many / are / potatoes / you / how
   _____?
5. aren't / sunglasses / why / your / you / wearing
   _____?
6. tonight / dinner / are / making / for / you / what
   _____?
7. Japanese / why / he / studying / is
   _____?

## 3 Present Continuous and Present Simple

Each sentence has a mistake. Find it and correct it.

1. What you doing?
   **What are you doing?**

2. Lin has breakfast right now.
   _____

3. They no coming to the party this evening.
   _____

4. I'm not understanding what you mean.
   _____

5. What do you do this weekend?
   _____

6. He's driving to work every day.
   _____

7. John don't like dancing.
   _____

## 4 Rob Phillips' vacation

Complete the text with the verbs in the box.

| | | | | |
|---|---|---|---|---|
| meet | ~~come~~ | finish | not work | love |
| travel | not like | start | like | fly |
| spend | camp | want | teach | have |

Rob Phillips is an English teacher at a language school in Seatttle. Students from all over the world (1) __come__ to study there. He (2) _____ grammar and conversation. He usually (3) _____ work at 9:00 and (4) _____ at 3:30. He (5) _____ his job because he (6) _____ a lot of people from other countries. But he (7) _____ now. He (8) _____ around Peru with a group of friends. They (9) _____ five days walking in the Andes. They (10) _____ in beautiful places every night, but Rob (11) _____ a problem. He (12) _____ walking, but he (13) _____ sleeping in a tent—he (14) _____ a real bed! They (15) _____ back to Seattle next week.

# going to

## 1 What are they going to buy for their vacation?

1 Match a line in **A** with a line in **B**.

| A | B |
|---|---|
| 1. Henry – Antarctica | a. ten water bottles |
| 2. I – the Alps | b. insect repellent |
| 3. Lynn and Pat – Peru | c. a very warm hat |
| 4. Jeff – the Sahara | d. new swimsuits |
| 5. Anne – the Amazon | e. an umbrella |
| 6. We – the Caribbean | f. a Spanish phrase book |
| 7. I – England | g. new ski boots |

2 Make sentences about what the people in Exercise 1 are going to buy.

1. __Henry's going to buy a very warm hat.__
2. _____
3. _____
4. _____
5. _____
6. _____
7. _____

## 2 Making negatives

Read the sentences about the past. Make negative sentences about the future.

1. I bought you lunch yesterday.

   __I'm not going to buy you lunch today.__

2. She swam two miles yesterday.

   _____

3. They caught the bus last week.

   _____

4. It snowed a lot last winter.

   _____

5. They won the last election.

   _____

6. I had a big breakfast yesterday.

   _____

7. Julia and Frank made lots of money last month.

   _____

## 3 Making questions

Sara and Mark are going to college next September. Make questions.

1. Where / they / live?

   __Where are they going to live?__

2. they / share / apartment?

   _____

3. What / Mark / study?

   _____

4. Sara / get / part-time job?

   _____

5. Where / they / buy books?

   _____

6. Mark / have enough money?

   _____

7. they / visit / parents?

   _____

# Present Perfect

## 1 Present Perfect affirmative and negative

What have Angela and Pedro done? Write sentences.

|  |  | Angela | Pedro |
|---|---|:---:|:---:|
| 1. | be / the U.S. | ✓ | ✓ |
| 2. | eat Thai food | ✓ | ✗ |
| 3. | ride / motorcycle | ✗ | ✓ |
| 4. | speak in public | ✗ | ✓ |
| 5. | see the president | ✓ | ✓ |
| 6. | break an arm | ✗ | ✓ |
| 7. | read *War and Peace* | ✓ | ✗ |
| 8. | study Portuguese | ✓ | ✓ |

1. **Angela and Pedro have both been to the U.S.**
2. **Angela has eaten Thai food, but Pedro hasn't.**
3. _____
4. _____
5. _____
6. _____
7. _____
8. _____

## 2 Present Perfect questions

Make questions with *ever*. Then answer the questions.

1. be / Turkey?
   **Have you ever been to Turkey?**
   **No, I haven't.**
2. drive / sports car ?
   _____
   _____
3. see anyone famous ?
   _____
   _____
4. lose your keys ?
   _____
   _____
5. make a cake ?
   _____
   _____
6. eat sushi ?
   _____
   _____
7. play basketball ?
   _____
   _____

## 3 This year or last year?

Match a line in **A** with lines in **B** and **C**.

| A | B | C |
|---|---|---|
| I've worn | $1,000 on clothes | |
| He flew | a new car | |
| She's written | this jacket every day | this year. |
| They spent | ten letters | last year. |
| I bought | $100 to charity | |
| I've broken | to Australia three times | |
| We've given | my leg twice | |

## 4 Present Perfect or Past Simple?

1 Read about Marcos and <u>underline</u> the correct verb form.

Marcos Santos is a chef. He (1) *started/has started* cooking when he (2) *has been/was* 15 years old. He (3) *has studied/studied* in a cooking school for the next three years, and then he (4) *got/has got* his first job, in a restaurant in Lyons. Now 33, he (5) *worked/has worked* all over France, and he (6) *just decided/has just decided* to open a restaurant in Los Angeles. (He (7) *hasn't thought/didn't think* of a name for it yet.) Four other top restaurants (8) *have opened/opened* there this year, but Marcos is optimistic. "My food (9) *was always/has always been* the best," he says. "In 1992 I (10) *cooked/have cooked* for the Italian President when he (11) *has come/came* to France, and he (12) *has told/told* me that it (13) *was/has been* the most delicious food outside Italy!"

2 Write questions about Marcos.

1. **What does he do** ?
   He's a chef.
2. _____ ?
   When he was 15.
3. _____ ?
   For three years.
4. _____ ?
   In a restaurant in Lyons.
5. _____ ?
   All over France.
6. _____ ?
   In Paris.
7. _____ ?
   Four.
8. _____ ?
   In 1992.

# Audio Scripts

## UNIT 2

### CD 10

| | |
|---|---|
| Int | Hello. Please sit down. |
| Diana | Thank you. |
| Int | What's your last name, please? |
| Diana | Gomez. |
| Int | How do you spell that? |
| Diana | G-O-M-E-Z. |
| Int | Thank you. And what's your first name? |
| Diana | Diana. |
| Int | And where are you from, Diana? |
| Diana | I'm from Colombia. |
| Int | What's your address in New York? |
| Diana | 161 Charles Street, Apartment 2, New York. |
| Int | And what's your phone number? |
| Diana | (212) 976-2454. |
| Int | (212) 976-2454? |
| Diana | Yes, that's right. |
| Int | Thank you. What's your job, Diana? Are you a student here? |
| Diana | Yes, I am. I'm a student of English. |
| Int | And how old are you? |
| Diana | I'm 20. |
| Int | Are you married, Diana? |
| Diana | No, I'm not. |
| Int | OK. Thank you very much. That's everything. Now … |

### CD 13

Hello. My name's David. I'm 74. I'm married. My wife's name is Mary. We have two children. Their names are Patrick and Shannon. Patrick is 48. His wife's name is Bonnie. Their children are Laura and Brian. Shannon is 43. Her husband's name is Ethan. They have a daughter, Heather, and a son, Connor. Heather is 15, and Connor is 13.

## Unit 3

### CD 16

| | |
|---|---|
| A | Who's that? |
| B | It's Hiroshi Fukuda. |
| A | Where does he come from? |
| B | Japan. |
| A | What does he do? |
| B | He's a television journalist. |
| A | Where does he live? |
| B | In Atlanta. |
| A | Where does he work? |
| B | At CNN. And he travels a lot. |
| A | Does he speak English and Japanese? |
| B | Yes, he does. And he speaks Korean, too. |
| A | Is he married? |
| B | Yes, he is. His wife's name is Nina. |
| A | How many children does he have? |
| B | Two. A son and a daughter. |
| A | What does he like doing in his free time? |
| B | Writing books and relaxing with his family. |

### CD 17

1. **Kurt** Kurt lives in Los Angeles, California. He speaks Spanish and English. He isn't married, and he doesn't have a dog. In his free time he likes going to the gym. He doesn't like listening to music. He likes his job very much. He's a pilot.

2. **Gloria** Gloria lives in the small town of Puerto Iguazu, Argentina. She speaks three foreign languages – English, Portuguese, and Spanish. She doesn't have a dog, but she has a cat. In her free time she likes listening to music and reading. She likes her job. She's a tour guide.

### CD 18

1. A Excuse me. Can you tell me the time, please?
   B Yes, of course. It's quarter after four.
   A Thank you very much.
2. A Excuse me. Can you tell me the time, please?
   B Yes. Um. It's twenty-five to five.
   A Oh, thanks.
3. A What time does your son get up?
   B About twenty after seven.
4. A Get up! It's late!
   B Wh … What time is it?
   A It's five to eight. Hurry up!
5. A What time does Rupert start work?
   B At nine o'clock, I think.
6. A And what time does he leave work?
   B About five-thirty.

## Unit 4

### CD 19

TA = travel agent, **MS** = Mr./Mrs. Smith

| | |
|---|---|
| TA | Good morning. Can I help you? |
| MS | Yes, please. My husband and I want to go on a winter vacation. |
| TA | Sure. Where do you want to go? |
| MS | Well. This is the problem. I like skiing and winter sports, but my husband doesn't. He wants to relax and sit in the sun, and the children … |
| TA | Children? How many children do you have? |
| MS | Two … two children, a son and a daughter. |
| TA | And how old are they? What do they like doing? |
| MS | Well. Our son's twelve. He loves all sports—skiing, swimming, football … Our daughter is sixteen. She doesn't like sports. She likes sunbathing, reading, drinking coffee … And she wants to practice her French. |
| TA | French! That gives me a good idea! I think I have the perfect winter vacation for your family! |

### CD 22

I live in Denver in the Western region of the United States. We have hot summers, and we often go to a pool to sunbathe and swim. But my favorite season is winter. It's cold and we usually have a lot of snow. We always go skiing in the Rocky Mountains. It's a beautiful place in the snow—all white and silver.

## UNIT 5

### CD 25

1. Start at the Internet cafe. Turn onto Main Street. Take the first street on the right. It's next to the bookstore. It's the music store.
2. Start at the bookstore. Turn onto South Street. Take the second street on the right. It's on the left. It's the drugstore.
3. Start at the train station. Go straight ahead. You're on South Street. It's on the left, next to the newsstand. It's the post office.
4. Start at the school. You're on Cambridge Street. Take the first street on the right. Go straight ahead. Take the second street on the left. It's on the left. It's the movie theater.

## UNIT 6

### CD 28

1. A How much is the camera?
   B It's only $60.
   A How much was it before?
   B It was $110.
   A Well, what a bargain!
2. A How much are the glasses?
   B They're only $39.99.
   A How much were they before?
   B They were $75.
   A Well, what a bargain!
3. A How much are the lamps?
   B They're only $40.
   A How much were they before?
   B They were $99.99.
   A Well, what a bargain!
4. A How much is the table?
   B It's only $69.99.
   A How much was it before?
   B It was $100.
   A Well, what a bargain!
5. A How much is the television?
   B It's only $350.
   A How much was it before?
   B It was $500.
   A Well, what a bargain!

### CD 30

1. **Female** Hello.
   **Paul** Hello. Can I speak to Jane, please?
   **Female** One moment. I'll get her.
   **Jane** Hello.
   **Paul** Jane, hi! It's Paul.
   **Jane** Paul!
   **Paul** Listen! Can you come to dinner at my house this Saturday?
   **Jane** Yes, of course. Sounds good!
   **Paul** Great! Is 8:00 OK?
   **Jane** Yes, that's fine.
   **Paul** See you on Saturday, then. Bye.
   **Jane** Bye, and thanks!
2. **Barry** Hello.
   **John** Hi, is this Barry?
   **Barry** Yes, it is.
   **John** It's John here. Listen, Barry. There's no football on Thursday evening.
   **Barry** Really?
   **John** Yeah. Mike's sick. Can you play on Friday evening?
   **Barry** Um … yes. Yes, I can.
   **John** Good! See you at 7:30. Bye.
   **Barry** Bye, and thanks for calling!
3. **Kate** Hello.
   **Meg** Kate, is that you?
   **Kate** Yes. Hi, Meg. How are you?
   **Meg** Oh, fine. Listen. Can you come to my house this evening?

| | |
|---|---|
| **Kate** | Yes. Why? |
| **Meg** | I can't do our homework! Can you? |
| **Kate** | I don't know. Is it difficult? |
| **Meg** | Yes! |
| **Kate** | OK. We can do it together, then. I can come at 6:00. |
| **Meg** | Great. See you then! |
| **Kate** | Bye! |

## UNIT 7

**CD 33**

Douglas Corrigan was a pilot from the United States. In 1938 he bought a small old plane for $150. He decided to fly from New York to Los Angeles. He looked at his map and planned the trip. But on the day of his flight, the weather was very bad. He couldn't see very well, and he went the wrong way. He turned left, not right. He flew across the Atlantic Ocean. He only had a map of the U.S. with him, and he didn't have any food or water.
He finally landed 28 hours and 13 minutes later. But he wasn't in Los Angeles, of course. He was in Dublin, Ireland. The people of Dublin were very surprised to see him. Lots of journalists came to interview him and the story of his amazing trip was in the newspapers the next day.
When Douglas Corrigan finally returned to New York, his friends had a big party for him. And after that, everyone always called him "Wrong Way Corrigan"!

## UNIT 8

**CD 37**

| | | |
|---|---|---|
| 1. | **A** | Guess what? Tom asked me to marry him last night! |
| | **B** | Wow! What did you say? |
| | **A** | I said "yes," of course! Look. He gave me an engagement ring! |
| | **B** | Show me! It's beautiful. Congratulations! |
| 2. | **A** | What time is it? |
| | **B** | It's nearly midnight. |
| | **A** | Ready, everybody? |
| | **All** | Happy New Year! |
| 3. | **A** | Mom! Dad! Wake up! |
| | **B** | What? It's only six o'clock. |
| | **A** | We want to go downstairs and open our presents under the tree! |
| | **B** | Oh, OK, then. Merry Christmas, sweetie! |
| | **A** | Merry Christmas, Mom! Merry Christmas, Dad! |
| 4. | **A** | Oh, look at all the mail that arrived this morning! Lots of cards for you! |
| | **B** | Wow! I'm four today, aren't I, Daddy? |
| | **A** | Yes, you are. And here's your present. Happy Birthday, Tommy! |
| 5. | **A** | It's ready, everybody! Come and sit down. |
| | **B** | Aunt Joy, you sit here, and Uncle Albert, you sit there. |
| | **A** | Raise your glasses, please. It's wonderful to see all the family here today. |
| | **B** | Yes. Happy Thanksgiving, everybody! |
| | **All** | Happy Thanksgiving! |

## UNIT 10

**CD 42**

| | |
|---|---|
| **A** | May I help you? |
| **B** | Yes, please. I'm looking for a shirt to go with these pants. |
| **A** | What color are you looking for? |
| **B** | I'm not sure. Pink or green, perhaps. |
| **A** | What about this one? |
| **B** | No. I don't like that pink. |

| | |
|---|---|
| **A** | OK. What about this one? It's a beautiful green. |
| **B** | Yes, that one's much better. Can I try it on? |
| **A** | Of course. There are the fitting rooms. |
| **A** | Is the size OK? |
| **B** | Yes, it's fine, but do you have another color? I'm not sure about this green. |
| **A** | No, we only have the pink one. Try it on. I'm sure it'll look nice. |
| **B** | Oh, OK. |
| **A** | I think that looks great. |
| **B** | Yes, I like it. It's a darker pink than I usually wear. But it's very nice. Thank you. I'll take it. |
| **A** | Good. That's 70 dollars. |
| **B** | Here's my card. |
| **A** | Thank you. Sign here. And here's your credit card back, and your shirt. Thank you very much. |
| **B** | Thank you. Bye. |

## UNIT 11

**CD 49**

| | |
|---|---|
| **Laura** | Mike, it's a beautiful day again. What should we do today? |
| **Mike** | Should we go to the beach again? I'd like to go swimming. |
| **Laura** | But we went to the beach yesterday, and the swimming pool the day before. Let's do something else today. Let's go into town! |
| **Mike** | But it's too hot for that. |
| **Laura** | No, it isn't. Not if we go early. Why don't we catch a bus into town after breakfast? We can look around the town center. And I'd like to look at some stores. |
| **Mike** | Oh, no—not shopping! |
| **Laura** | I just want to buy some postcards and some souvenirs. I'll be quick, I promise. |
| **Mike** | OK. Then let's have an early lunch in a restaurant in the town center. |
| **Laura** | OK. Good idea. We can practice speaking Spanish! And we can get back to the hotel before it's too hot. |
| **Mike** | And then we can go to the beach and go swimming! |
| **Laura** | Oh, OK. Let's do that. I'll get my hat, and let's go down for breakfast. |
| **Mike** | Let's go! |

## UNIT 12

**CD 52**

| | |
|---|---|
| **Bob** | Well, So-young, you've checked in your luggage. What's your flight number? |
| **So-young** | Um … let's see … it's Flight 172. Look, it's on the monitor. It says "wait in lounge." |
| **Becky** | Do you have a window seat? |
| **So-young** | Yes, I do. Look, seat number A42. |
| **Bob** | Do you have everything, So-young? |
| **So-young** | I think so. My ticket, my boarding pass, my passport. They're all here in my bag. |
| **Julie** | Good. Now, you're going to call us when you get home, aren't you? |
| **So-young** | Of course! Thank you, Julie. Thanks, Bob. It's been wonderful. |
| **Becky** | I'll miss you, So-young. Write to me. |
| **So-young** | Of course! I'll miss you too, Becky—lots! Give my love to James. And visit me in Seoul when you can. |
| **Becky** | I'm coming in the summer, definitely. |

| | |
|---|---|
| **Info** | Flight 172 to Seoul, boarding now, gate 11. |
| **Bob** | That's your flight, So-young. |
| **So-young** | Oh, good-bye, everyone. Thanks for everything. I've had a fantastic time in New York. |
| **All** | Bye, So-young. Have a great flight! Bye! |

This page has been left blank.

# SPOTLIGHT ON TESTING

### Giving personal information

Speakers often say who they are and what they do. This is called *personal information*. Listen for details about speakers. Some questions in listening tests ask you for this.

**1 Listening for personal information**

AUDIO FILE 🔊 Listen to or read the conversation. Check (✔) the true statements.

☐ Jenny is not from a big city.

☐ Mark does not like big campuses.

☐ Mark and Jenny live in the same dorm.

| | |
|---|---|
| **Mark** Hi. My name's Mark. | **Mark** Yeah. In Condon Hall. How about you? |
| **Jenny** Nice to meet you, Mark. I'm Jenny. | **Jenny** I'm in Anders Hall. It looks OK. |
| **Mark** Hi Jenny. Are you a freshman, too? | **Mark** Have you seen much of the dorm? |
| **Jenny** Yeah. My first day here! It's scary. | **Jenny** No. I haven't even met my roommate. |
| **Mark** Scary? What do you mean? | **Mark** Are you nervous? Do you know anything about her? |
| **Jenny** Well, the university is so big! | **Jenny** Not much. I know she's from India. |
| **Mark** Yeah, this is a big campus. But I like it. | **Mark** India! Cool. She's probably lost on campus, too. |
| **Jenny** So do I. Still… I'm from a small town. | **Jenny** Maybe. In fact, maybe she's here at the new students' meeting. |
| **Mark** Oh, really? Where? | **Mark** Maybe. |
| **Jenny** A town called Springport. It's in Ohio. | **Jenny** The speaker is starting now. I'll talk to you later. |
| **Mark** Hey, I'm from Ohio, too. Wow! | **Mark** Yeah. See you later. |
| **Jenny** That's incredible. Where in Ohio? | |
| **Mark** Well, Columbus, near Ohio State University. I've seen big campuses before. | |
| **Jenny** Yeah. I'm sure. So, do you live in a dorm here on campus? | |

### Working with forms

Sometimes people fill out forms. A form has spaces to give written information. Some tests ask you to read forms. Before a test, you often have to fill out a form yourself.

**2 Personal information on a form**

AUDIO FILE 🔊 Listen to or read the conversation again. Fill out the form with Jenny's information.

First name: _____

Hometown: _____

Dorm on campus: _____

Strategies for taking the: TOEFL® Test  TOEIC® Test  IELTS™ Test

## 3 Working with information on a form

Read the form. Circle the letter of the correct answer.

1. Before coming to the university, Dennis lived in ___.
   a. Iowa    b. East Fee Hall    c. the Biology Department

2. Dennis' ID number is ___.
   a. 52231    b. 1792    c. PZ4835

3. Dennis' home telephone number in Harper is ___.
   a. (641) 555-9092    b. (614) 555-0123    c. 6-2091

---

# Barton University Student Information Form

Date ___May 17, 2010___                     Student ID number ___PZ4835___

Student name ___Dennis Patrick Ford___

Home address ___1792 Brooklyn Drive___

City / Town ___Harper___        State ___Iowa___        ZIP ___52231___

Home Phone ___(641) 555-9092___        Cell phone ___(614) 555-0123___

Campus address ___144 East Fee Hall___

Campus phone ___726-2091___

Date of birth ___February 10, 1993___

Academic Status

Date admitted ___May 16, 2010___        GPA: ___Not yet known___

Department ___Biology___        Graduation date: ___Not yet known___

---

## 4 Check your understanding

Read the form again. Check (✔) each true statement.

1. ___ Dennis is from a town called "Iowa."

2. ___ Dennis has three phone numbers.

3. ___ Dennis lives on the university campus.

4. ___ Dennis was born in 1993.

> In a speaking test, if the tester asks you to introduce yourself, keep it short. Say your name. You can also say where you are from. Don't say more unless the tester asks.

## 5 Skills in review

Look at Exercise 3 on page 3 of the Workbook. Make sentences like those for Mark, Jenny, or Dennis.

# Unit 2 | Pronouns and Possessive nouns

A *pronoun* (*he/him*, *they/them*, etc.) refers to a noun. For example, in the sentences *Bob has a book. He dropped it.*, the pronoun *He* refers to *Bob*. *It* refers to *book*. Some tests ask about the meaning of pronouns.

## 1 Using pronouns

Read the e-mail. What noun does each pronoun refer to? Fill in the chart.

| Sentence from the e-mail | Pronoun | Refers to |
|---|---|---|
| 1. It has a lot of big old trees. | it | *campus* |
| 2. They seem hard. | they | |
| 3. If we get some free time, I'd like to visit her town. | we | |
| 4. Zara says he makes great food. | he | |
| 5. I miss them a lot. | them | |

**To:** Mike Bates
**From:** Monica Chen
**Date:** September 3
**Subject:** Hi… from Singapore!

Hi Mike,

I'm just writing to say hi. I'm in Singapore now. It's hot, but my room has air conditioning. How's the weather in Boston?

My new university's campus is beautiful. It has a lot of big old trees. Some of the buildings are old too, but most of them are newer. They say it is Asia's best engineering university. My classes started two days ago. They seem hard. My math professor's favorite saying is, "Work, work, work." I am tired already!

My roommate is from Malaysia. Her name is Zara. She's from a town called Kuantan. It's near the sea and has great beaches. I'd like to visit her town some day. Zara's mother is a teacher and her dad owns a small restaurant. Zara says he makes great food. Her favorite food is called *roti*. It's a kind of flat bread. She says her father makes Malaysia's best *roti*.

Are you back in school yet? When do your classes start? Did you visit your family this summer? How are they? It was hard to leave my parents in Hong Kong. I miss them a lot. I want to go home during winter vacation. OK. I'll stop writing now and start studying. E-mail me when you get a chance. Bye!

Monica

Strategies for taking the:   TOEFL® Test   TOEIC® Test   IELTS™ Test

*Possessive nouns* tell who owns something. They usually end in 's: *Lena's chair* = The chair belongs to Lena. Sometimes the possessive noun comes after *of*: *a chair of Lena's* = Many chairs belong to Lena and this is one of them.

**2 Understanding possessive nouns**

Read these sentences from the e-mail in Exercise 1. Circle the possessive nouns.

1. My new university's campus is beautiful.

2. My math professor's favorite saying is, "Work, work, work."

3. She says her father makes Malaysia's best *roti*.

**3 Practice with possessive nouns**

AUDIO FILE 🔊 Listen to or read the conversation. Then look at the list below. Whose things are they? Circle the correct answer.

| | | | |
|---|---|---|---|
| 1. the wedding | Dan | Fred | John |
| 2. the name John | Tina's brother | Tina's friend | Tina's father |
| 3. a family from Chicago | Tina | Ben | Mary |
| 4. a baseball cap | Dan | Ben | Steve |

| | | | |
|---|---|---|---|
| **Fred** | Tina. That's a nice picture. | **Tina** | That's right. This is Ben and this is Mary. |
| **Tina** | Thanks, Fred. This is my family. The picture is from my brother's wedding. | **Fred** | Where are they from? |
| **Fred** | So, he's the guy in the black suit? | **Tina** | Ben's family is from Ohio. Mary's family is from Chicago. |
| **Tina** | Right. My brother's name is Dan. | **Fred** | Who is this guy? Is he wearing a cap to a wedding? |
| **Fred** | What's his wife's name? | | |
| **Tina** | Sue. | **Tina** | That's my youngest brother. Steve's baseball cap is in all of our family pictures. |
| **Fred** | So, who are these other people? | | |
| **Tina** | These are my parents. My dad's name is John and my mother's is Brenda. | **Fred** | Why? Does it have special meaning to him? |
| **Fred** | And I bet these are Sue's parents. | **Tina** | His college's name is on it. Maybe he's really proud of that. |

**4 Check your understanding**

AUDIO FILE 🔊 Listen to or read the conversation in Exercise 3 again. Write *T* for true or *F* for false.

1. ____ Tina just got married.

2. ____ Fred's brother is in the picture.

3. ____ Tina's mother was at the wedding.

4. ____ Tina has more than one brother.

> To answer a pronoun question on a test, look for nouns that match the pronoun. Is the pronoun male, female, or neither? Is it singular or plural?

**5 Skills in review**

Look at Exercise 12 on page 9 of the Workbook. Now look at the conversation between Mark and Jenny. In the conversation, find words where 's = possession.

# Unit 3 | Regular activities

*Present simple* verbs show the things people usually do. For example, "I write reports" means "I often or usually write reports." Some test questions are about things people usually do in their jobs, for fun, etc.

## 1 Understanding what people usually do

AUDIO FILE 🔊 Listen to or read the conversation. What do these workers usually do? Check (✓) every statement that is true.

1. ☐ Waiters bring food.

2. ☐ Ken cooks food.

3. ☐ Dining hall workers clear tables.

4. ☐ Hall attendants wash dishes.

5. ☐ Hall attendants keep people safe.

6. ☐ Hall monitors stop fights.

| | |
|---|---|
| **Ms. Henner** | Hi, Ken. My assistant Janet gives me interesting job applications. She gave me yours. |
| **Ken** | Thanks, Ms. Henner. I'd like to work here at Wilson Hall. |
| **Ms. Henner** | We have some jobs open. What job experience do you have? |
| **Ken** | Now, I'm a waiter at a restaurant. I serve food to customers. I also help wash dishes. |
| **Ms. Henner** | We need workers in our dining hall. They clear tables and wash dishes. |
| **Ken** | Actually, Ms. Henner, I'd like to try a different job. |
| **Ms. Henner** | Okay. We need hall attendants, too. |
| **Ken** | What do hall attendants do? |
| **Ms. Henner** | They keep the hall safe. Sometimes they keep dangerous people away from the dorm. |
| **Ken** | That sounds interesting. |

| | |
|---|---|
| **Ms. Henner** | Also, sometimes they stop fights between students. |
| **Ken** | I can do that. |
| **Ms. Henner** | Janet supervises our attendants. She says stopping fights can be hard. Do you have experience doing that? |
| **Ken** | In high school, I was a hall monitor. |
| **Ms. Henner** | What does that mean? |
| **Ken** | A hall monitor keeps the halls quiet. Sometimes a monitor stops fights. |
| **Ms. Henner** | That sounds great. When can you start? |
| **Ken** | My restaurant work ends on August 15. |
| **Ms. Henner** | Good. See Janet. She helps new employees. |
| **Ken** | Thanks a lot, Ms. Henner. |

When you listen to a conversation, listen for differences between people. What does Person A do? Does Person B do different things? Test questions may ask you about these differences.

## 2 Understanding who does an action

AUDIO FILE 🔊 Listen to or read the conversation again. Which person does it? Write *J* for Janet or *K* for Ken.

1. ____ gives Ms. Henner job applications

2. ____ works in a restaurant

3. ____ supervises hall attendants

4. ____ wants a hall attendant job

Strategies for taking the: TOEFL® Test   TOEIC® Test   IELTS™ Test

## 3 Who does each job?

Read the article. Who does each job? Write the names in the chart.

| Job | Who does it |
|---|---|
| 1. controlling a plane during the flight | |
| 2. making sure customers can get tickets online | |
| 3. checking tickets as people get on the plane | |
| 4. helping people find places for their bags | |

## Career Choices in the Air

Most air travelers know about a pilot's work. The pilot controls the airplane. But many other people also help make your flight safe and comfortable. Airline companies offer many careers.

Several people help customers get tickets. A very important job in airlines is the Web Manager. This person makes sure that the company's website is working well. Can customers find flights, make their reservations online, and get e-tickets? Fifteen years ago, airlines did not need good websites. Now, most airline customers book their flights online.

Airlines also have gate agents. They work in airports, where customers get on the plane. They solve last-minute problems. They also call passengers to the plane and check each ticket. On the plane, an air traveler sees flight attendants. They help people to their seats and find places for the bags people have carried onto the plane. A flight attendant tells travelers about safety during the flight. Later, the flight attendants offer drinks, and sometimes food, to the travelers.

During the flight, the pilot is helped by a co-pilot. The co-pilot checks important aspects of the flight—speed, height, direction, and so on. The co-pilot also helps the pilot communicate with controllers on the ground.

For more information on an airline career, try going to an airline's website. Most have a "careers" section.

## 4 Check your understanding

Read the article again. Circle the best word or phrase in each sentence.

1. A (Web Manager / pilot) makes sure the website is working well.

2. (Gate agents / Flight attendants) work on the airplane.

3. (Flight attendants / co-pilots) offer drinks to customers.

4. The (co-pilot / flight attendant) helps the pilot communicate with controllers.

Some listening tests let you take notes. Try dividing your notepaper into one part for each speaker. This will help you remember facts about each speaker.

## 5 Skills in review

Look at the yes/no questions in Section 8 on page 15 of the Workbook. Write your own yes/no questions about people who work for an airline. For example, a question could be, "Do Web Managers help people get tickets?" Write answers to your questions.

# Unit 4 | Favorites

### Positive and negative verbs

Some statements have *positive* verbs, and others have *negative* verbs. Look for these differences in reading. Especially look for *not* or *n't*, which are part of negative verbs. Many test questions ask about positive and negative verbs.

## 1 Understanding positive and negative verbs

Read the e-mails. Circle the correct verb in these sentences.

1. Kari (has / doesn't have) a new job.

2. Kari (can / cannot) visit Margaret.

3. Margaret (bought / did not buy) a new piano.

4. Margaret (drives / does not drive) her mother to the doctor.

| To: | Margaret Stone |
| From: | Kari Allen |
| Date: | May 12 |
| Subject: | my visit |

Hi Margaret,

Sorry I haven't e-mailed in a while. I got a new job, so I've been busy. I am now a manager at a pet store in Brookwood Mall. We have mostly small pets like birds and hamsters. We have some cats, too. They're my favorite and especially beautiful! I like this job, but I have bad news. Unfortunately, I can't visit you at the end of the month. I was really looking forward to it, but I have to work. Please don't be mad at me! I asked for the time off but couldn't get it.

| To: | Kari Allen |
| From: | Margaret Stone |
| Date: | May 13 |
| Subject: | your visit |

Hi Kari,

Congratulations on the new job! About the visit: that's too bad. I was looking forward to it, too. You're my best friend! You know how pianos are my favorite instrument? I bought a new piano, and I want you to see it—and hear it. It's great. Unfortunately, I can't visit you either. As you know, my mom broke her leg and I have to take care of her. She can't drive right now, so I have to take her shopping, take her to the doctor, and so on. But the doctor says she can drive next month. Maybe we can get together then?

### Describing favorites

Writing or speaking tests may ask for information about something you like very much—your favorite movie, your favorite sport, etc. Listen to other people talk about their favorites. Learn important vocabulary like *most of all*, *best*, *especially*, etc.

Strategies for taking the:    TOEFL® Test    TOEIC® Test    IELTS™ Test

**2 My favorite things**

Read the e-mails again. Write an answer to each question.

1. What are Kari's favorite pets? _____

2. Who is Margaret's favorite friend? _____

3. What is Margaret's favorite musical instrument? _____

**3 Listening for favorites**

AUDIO FILE 🔊 Listen to or read the interview. Fill in Tom and Dana's favorites.

**Tom's favorites**    Sports: _____    Movies: _____

　　　　　　　　　　Cooking: _____

**Dana's favorites**    Sports: _____    Movies: _____

　　　　　　　　　　Cooking: _____

| | | | |
|---|---|---|---|
| Interviewer | I'm here with Tom Coleman of Coleman Computers and Dana Hill of Best Communications. Hi, Tom. Hi, Dana. | Dana | My family and I have a movie night every week. Mysteries are the best! I love guessing the ending. |
| Tom | Hi. Thanks for inviting me. | Tom | I love movies, too! For me it's action. Give me movies with lots of excitement. |
| Dana | Hi. Glad to be here. | | |
| Interviewer | You're busy people. Do you ever get time for fun? | Interviewer | Well, that's interesting. |
| Tom | Sure. I work hard, but I also play hard. | Tom | Let me add another thing. I like to cook. It lets me be creative. |
| Dana | You've got to have fun! | Interviewer | What do you usually cook? |
| Interviewer | What do you like to do? | Tom | Mostly Italian food. |
| Tom | My favorite sport is biking. I love the exercise. Most days, I bike to work. | Dana | I cook for fun, too. I'm really interested in Indian food. |
| Dana | Biking's good, but my favorite is skiing. | Interviewer | Well, that's great! Thanks to you both for your time. |
| Interviewer | How about movies, DVDs, that kind of thing? | Dana | Thank you. It was lots of fun. |
| | | Tom | Bye. |

**4 Check your understanding**

AUDIO FILE 🔊 Listen to or read the interview again. Write *T* for true or *F* for false.

1. ____ Tom often rides his bike to work.

2. ____ Dana doesn't watch many movies.

3. ____ Both Tom and Dana think cooking is fun.

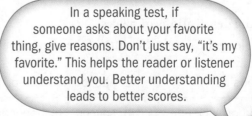

In a speaking test, if someone asks about your favorite thing, give reasons. Don't just say, "it's my favorite." This helps the reader or listener understand you. Better understanding leads to better scores.

**5 Skills in review**

Look at Exercise 6 on page 19 of the Workbook. Make your own sentences about what you like to do or don't like to do. Use *always, never, sometimes, usually,* and *often*.

# Unit 5 | Describing places

*There is/there are* in descriptions of places

Reading or listening questions sometimes ask you what is in a place. Use *there is* and *there are* to talk about where something is. Use *is* with singular things. Use *are* with plural things.

**1  Welcome to Camptown College**

Read the information about the college. Fill in the blanks with *there is* or *there are*.

1. _____ a beautiful campus at Camptown.

2. At Camptown, _____ 11 varsity sports for women.

3. _____ no part-time teachers at Camptown.

4. In the library, _____ an area for quiet study.

---

**i Internet Search**  ⎯ ☐ ✕

Address `http://www.camptowncollege.com`  ▼ Go

# Welcome to Camptown College

There is a great college waiting for you in Florida: Camptown. Our campus is beautiful. There are four lakes on the campus. There is also some great shopping 40 miles away in Orlando. There are many parks and tourist attractions near campus as well.

**Teachers**

Camptown teachers are interested in every student. Our classes are small. There is one teacher for every 13 students. Every teacher works full time and is always available to help.

**Athletics**

There are 11 varsity sports for women and 10 for men. Our women's basketball team won the national championship in 2008 and 2009. Some students like to play just for fun. For them, we

have recreational teams in soccer, basketball, and even rugby.

**Library**

Camptown's new library is the largest in the southeastern U.S. One part of the building has four floors of quiet study. Another has special rooms for group study. A room in our main lobby is full of books by Camptown teachers. Camptown students can also access more than 500 online databases for free.

---

**2  Understanding descriptions of places**

Read the article again. Circle the letter of the phrase that is NOT true.

| | |
|---|---|
| 1. The campus . . . | a. has four lakes.   b. is in Orlando.   c. is in Florida. |
| 2. Campus sports include . . . | a. soccer.   b. national basketball champions.   c. mostly men's teams. |
| 3. The library has . . . | a. 500 books.   b. more than one wing.   c. a special room for books by teachers. |

Strategies for taking the:   TOEFL® Test    TOEIC® Test    IELTS™ Test

Prepositions like *on*, *in*, or *next to* help describe exactly where something is. Detail questions on English language tests often ask about this. Look for the prepositions as you listen or read.

**3  Prepositions showing where something is**

AUDIO FILE 🔊 Listen to or read the lecture. Circle the correct preposition.

1. Most buildings in Petra are carved *in / behind* solid rock.

2. Tall pillars stand *next to / under* the fake roofs.

3. A small river goes *in front of / through* the area near Petra.

# Lecture: The Lost City of Petra

Today I'd like to talk about a marvelous old city called Petra. It is in western Jordan. Visitors to Petra travel through very dry land. The mountains of the area are rocky, with no trees. Most people travel along and wonder, "How could anyone live here?" Then, suddenly, they come to a deep crack in the rocks. They can look over the edge, and . . . wow! There is a beautiful ancient city below them. It is cut out of stone.

Almost all the buildings of Petra are cut into high rock walls. The rooms inside have smooth floors and pictures on the walls. The outsides of the buildings look like ancient Greek temples or other important buildings. The outlines of fake roofs are cut into the rock. Tall pillars under them hold these "roofs" up.

Petra was made by a people known as the Nabateans. They were not Greeks, but they had a lot of contact with Greeks. That's why their buildings used the Greek style. These people made most of Petra's buildings in about 100 BCE. Why did they build here? Well, the deep cracks gave the Nabateans shade. Much of the day, the desert sun was behind the rock walls. Also, for part of the year, a small river runs through the area. The Nabateans could collect water to use all year.

**4  Check your understanding**

AUDIO FILE 🔊 Listen to or read the lecture again. Write the correct preposition in each blank.

1. Petra is _____ the western part of Jordan.

2. Visitors look into a deep crack in the rock. _____ them there is a beautiful city.

3. The Nabateans got shade because the sun was often _____ the rock walls.

**5  Skills in review**

Look at the map on page 25 of the Workbook. Write sentences using *there is/there are* and prepositions to describe the town shown on the map.

> Test questions often ask about *facts*. First, find the key words in the question. Then, look quickly for the key words in the reading. The answer is usually near the key words.

# Unit 6 | Abilities and forms of *can*

## Abilities

*Abilities* are things you can do. *I can walk to school* means "I have the ability to walk to school." Some ability words are *can* and *could*. Reading and listening tests sometimes ask about abilities. Who can do something? What can he or she do?

## 1 Talking about abilities

**AUDIO FILE** 🔊 Listen to or read the telephone conversation. What can the speakers do? Check (✓) each true statement.

1. ☐ Mark can help Jenny move things.
2. ☐ Jenny can't drive a pickup truck.
3. ☐ Jenny can understand her landlord's notes.
4. ☐ Jenny can't call Mark later.

**Mark**  Hello?

**Jenny**  Hi, Mark?

**Mark**  Hi, Jenny. What's up?

**Jenny**  Not much. I'm just calling to say hello and… well… to ask something. Can you help me with something?

**Mark**  I'll try. What do you need?

**Jenny**  Well, I'm moving into a new apartment and I need help moving some heavy things.

**Mark**  OK. I can get a couple of guys to help.

**Jenny**  Can you? That would be great.

**Mark**  Sure. Do you have a truck or something?

**Jenny**  Yeah. I can get my dad's pickup truck. It should be big enough.

**Mark**  Good. Can you drive it OK?

**Jenny**  Of course I can! You think I can't drive a pickup truck?

**Mark**  No, no… That's not it. Never mind. Sorry.

**Jenny**  That's OK. One other thing… I can't understand some things at the apartment, like the heating and air-conditioning….

**Mark**  Didn't your landlord leave notes about that?

**Jenny**  Yeah, but a lot of it is in Spanish. I can't speak Spanish. But you can, right?

**Mark**  Yeah, I can probably read the directions.

**Jenny**  Good. Can you meet me at the apartment tomorrow after work?

**Mark**  Sure. Where is it?

**Jenny**  It's at… Oh, sorry. I have another call coming in from my mom. Can I call you back and give you the address?

**Mark**  No problem. You can reach me here until about 9:00.

## 2 Timed speaking practice

Some speaking tests ask you to talk for a minute about something. Practice speaking quickly. Answer each question in 60 seconds or less. Use a watch to time yourself.

1. Why did Jenny call Mark?

2. Talk about a time when you needed help from someone.

3. Mark can help Jenny because he speaks Spanish. Have you ever used your language ability to help someone?

Strategies for taking the:   TOEFL® Test   TOEIC® Test   IELTS™ Test

*Can* is present; *could* is past. The negative forms are *can't* and *couldn't*. On tests, you must often understand when an action happened and who was—or wasn't—able to do it.

### 3 Practicing forms of *can*

Read the article. Circle the correct word in each statement.

1. Light from the sun (can / can't) push space sails.

2. Scientists (can / could) build space sails long ago.

3. In 2005, a rocket (could / couldn't) put a space sail into space.

4. Now, space scientists (can't / couldn't) easily get money from governments.

## Space Sailing

Someday, people from Earth may go sailing in space. This is not just a dream. Scientists can already build large ships with space sails. The sails are made of thin, very light cloth. They catch light from the sun. The energy from this light can push the vehicles along. Regular space ships carry a lot of fuel. They can't travel very far because the fuel is so heavy. Space sailing can solve this problem. Their only fuel is light.

Space sailing is not new. Scientists from Russia and the United States built space sails long ago. They tried to shoot a space-sail vehicle into space in 2005 but failed. Their rocket couldn't fly high enough. The vehicle fell back to Earth.

A big problem for space sailing is money. In earlier times, governments were excited about space travel. Space programs could get government money. Now, there is not as much money for things like space sailing. There are other problems, too. Over time, a space-sailing ship can get too far from the sun. It will lose light and stop. Scientists can solve this problem, but only with a lot of effort. They can put lasers near faraway planets like Neptune. There, light from the lasers can keep the space sails going. However, the faraway lasers cost a lot of money—even more than space sails.

### 4 Check your understanding

Read the article again. Circle the correct answer.

1. In the 2005 space shot, what failed?
   a. a space sail    b. a rocket

2. Who gave money for space sails?
   a. companies    b. governments

3. What can push space sails that are far from the sun?
   a. laser light    b. sunlight

> The word *can* is hard for many people to hear. Practice hearing it in everyday conversations. Practice saying it in full sentences, like *I can sing* or *Ships can sail*.

### 5 Skills in review

Look at Exercise 1 on page 26 of the Workbook. Now look at the conversation between Mark and Jenny in Exercise 1 above. Write sentences about Mark and Jenny like those in Exercise 1 on page 26.

# Unit 7 | Dates and time expressions

Words like *yesterday*, *today*, and *tomorrow* tell you when something happens. Some reading questions ask about when something happens. Look for these words. They might lead you to the answer.

## 1 Using time expressions

Read the article about the museum. Show time order from the past to the future. Write numbers from 1 (earliest) to 4 (latest).

a. ＿＿＿ Getting a big gift from Fred Norman

b. ＿＿＿ Being named the Middle State Museum

c. ＿＿＿ Getting a part of the Berlin Wall

d. ＿＿＿ Opening a science and technology section

## Museum Gets Big Gift

The Smith Museum in Daytown got a big gift yesterday. Fred Norman, a rich businessman, gave $15.2 million to the museum. This gift is going to help the museum build a new section for science and technology. The new section will open two years from now.

"This is a major gift," said Ben Thomas, the museum's president. "We are ready to start building tomorrow." The new section is going to show some of the greatest inventions of the modern world. "We are going to show important objects like early DVD players and video games. People of all ages find these things interesting."

The Smith Museum has many special sections. The newest one is a modern history exhibit. It includes a brick taken from the Berlin Wall and a copy of the first Harry Potter book signed by author J. K. Rowling. The science and technology section is going to be the largest in the state.

The Smith Museum started as the Middle State Museum. Thirty years later, it got its new name and moved to a building in downtown Daytown. It earns some of its money by selling tickets to its special shows. However, it gets most of its money from the city of Daytown and from rich supporters. The gift from Norman is the largest one ever received by the museum.

## 2 Check your understanding

Read the article again. Circle the letter of the best answer.

1. Fred Norman is...   a. a rich person   b. the museum's president

2. The museum gets most of its money from...   a. the city   b. selling tickets

3. J. K. Rowling...   a. writes books   b. invents things

A date is a day when something happened. The name of a date usually includes a month and a number. Some ways of saying the date July 3 are: (1) "July third," (2) "the third of July."

Strategies for taking the:   TOEFL® Test   TOEIC® Test   IELTS™ Test

## 3 Understanding how speakers say dates

AUDIO FILE 🔊 Listen to or read the lecture. Circle the correct date.

1. When did the wind turbine start working?
   a. August 1    b. September 10

2. When is the new bike path going to open?
   a. September 12    b. September 10

3. When did the Johnson Building let people visit the garden on its roof?
   a. July 8    b. July 4

| | |
|---|---|
| **Jenny** | I don't think our town does enough to protect nature. |
| **Mark** | What about our wind turbine? It makes electricity from wind power. |
| **Jenny** | I haven't seen that. |
| **Mark** | Well, they just put it up at the college. It started working on August first. |
| **Jenny** | That's good. And we do have nice bike paths. |
| **Mark** | And a new one is going to open on the tenth of September. |
| **Jenny** | I thought it was September twelfth. |
| **Mark** | Uh . . . no. That's a Monday. They're going to open it on a Saturday. For the weekend. |
| **Jenny** | OK, but we should also do more. |
| **Mark** | We have a green building—you know, one that helps keep the environment safe. |
| **Jenny** | We do? |
| **Mark** | Sure. The Johnson Building. |

**Jenny** Now I remember. They put a garden on the roof. I think it was in two thousand eight.

**Mark** Yeah. They let people visit it on the fourth of July.

**Jenny** OK. I was unfair. We do help nature in some ways.

**Mark** And different people do different things.

**Jenny** Yeah. I recycle newspapers. I never throw them in the garbage.

**Mark** Me, too. I started doing that . . . well, I can't remember when.

**Jenny** I think they started picking up recycled things about ten years ago.

**Mark** Well, then I was just a little kid. I started later than that!

**Jenny** I mean, maybe your family started doing it then.

**Mark** Yeah, you're right. I think we did.

## 4 Check your understanding

AUDIO FILE 🔊 Listen to or read the lecture again. Write *T* for true or *F* for false.

1. ____ A wind turbine produces electricity.

2. ____ The green building has a garden on its roof.

3. ____ Mark and Jenny both recycle newspapers.

## 5 Skills in review

Look at Exercise 6 on page 31 of the Workbook. Make questions and answers like these for the article about the museum in Exercise 1 or the conversation about protecting nature in Exercise 3 above.

> In listening tests, it is important to tell the difference between years and dates. For help, listen for prepositions. Before the number for a date, you often hear *on*. Before a year, you often hear *in*.

### Time expressions 2: *earlier, before, specific years*

Unit 7 was about some words that show time. Some more words like this are *earlier, before,* and the names of years. Look for these words when answering time questions about a reading or listening passage.

**1 Using expressions to understand time**

Read the article. The line shows times from the past to now. When did each thing happen? Write the number next to the event.

PAST    1    2    3    4    NOW

a. ____ Black-and-white TVs stop using non-electric parts.

b. ____ Most homes in the U.S. have a TV.

c. ____ Philo Farnsworth invents his TV.

d. ____ Scientists first send pictures over electric wires.

## The First TV

Many people think Philo Farnsworth invented the first TV. This is not exactly true. Many people helped invent TV. Farnsworth made his TV in 1927. Many other inventions came earlier and later.

Even in the 1860s and 1870s, scientists sent pictures over electric wires. Famous inventors like Thomas Edison and Alexander Graham Bell worked on TV in the 1880s. They looked for ways to send sound and pictures together. The name "television" was first used at the Paris World's Fair in 1900.

In the early days, some televisions were not all electric. Some used moving wheels. By the early 1920s, this changed. All black-and-white TVs (without color pictures) used only electric parts. Vladimir Zworkin, a Russian living in the United States, invented many of these new parts. He and

Farnsworth worked in different places. They did not know each other. They did not know about each other's work. Actually, they both invented modern, all-electric TVs at the same time without knowing it.

TVs became more common in the early 1930s. In many places, like England (1930) and Mexico (1935), the first TV broadcasts came from the government. In the U.S., a university sent out the first shows (1933). Through the 1940s and 1950s, private TV companies grew in the U.S. The government made rules to control the companies, but TV shows did not come from the government. By 1960, most homes in the United States had at least one TV. Many shows were still in black and white. By the late 1960s this changed. Most shows were in color.

### Years in listening passages

The number of a year is usually said in two parts: (1) the first two numbers and (2) the second two. For example, *1994* is said "nineteen ninety-four." Sometimes, a year is named only by its second two numbers: *1994* might be called "ninety-four."

Strategies for taking the:   TOEFL® Test   TOEIC® Test   IELTS™ Test

## 2 How to say the names of years

Here are some years from the article. Say each year. Use the correct pattern.

a. 1927　　b. 1935　　c. 1960

## 3 Understanding years in speech

AUDIO FILE 🔊 Read or listen to the conversation. The years are not written in numbers. They are written in full words. Write the year next to each event. Two of the years will not be used.

| Years | Events |
|---|---|
| 1979<br>1984<br>1985<br>1986<br>1990<br>1993 | 1. _____ Megan's parents got married.<br>2. _____ Megan's parents became neighbors.<br>3. _____ Megan was born.<br>4. _____ Megan's parents graduated from college. |

**Jason** Hi, Megan. Hey, nice dress! What's going on?

**Megan** Thanks, Jason. It's my mom and dad's anniversary. We're going out to dinner.

**Jason** That's nice. How long have they been married?

**Megan** Like, forever! They got married in nineteen ninety.

**Jason** Well, that's not as long as my parents. Nineteen eighty-six for them.

**Megan** Yeah. A long time. It's kind of cool about my parents. They were actually friends as kids.

**Jason** Neighbors? Like us?

**Megan** Well, at first they just went to school together, in the seventies.

**Jason** Elementary school? Like when they were ten or eleven?

**Megan** Right. Then my mom's family moved next door to my dad's in, uh, nineteen seventy-nine.

**Jason** So they fell in love as teenagers?

**Megan** Not at first, no. They were just friends. Then they both went away to college—but to the same place!

**Jason** That's weird. So they're in another town, and they don't know anyone else and…

**Megan** So they became closer and, well, you know.

**Jason** So they graduated in like, eighty-four or eighty-five.

**Megan** Eighty-five.

**Jason** You must have been born soon after that.

**Megan** Yeah, not long. I was born in nineteen ninety-three. January.

**Jason** So you're younger than me. About two years younger, in fact. I guess I never knew that.

**Megan** You were born in ninety-one? Oh. That's interesting.

## 4 Check your understanding

Read the conversation again. Write *T* for true or *F* for false.

1. ____ Megan's parents got married four years after Jason's.

2. ____ Megan is older than Jason.

3. ____ Megan's parents went to college together.

4. ____ Megan and Jason are neighbors.

## 5 Skills in review

Look at Exercise 6 on page 36 of the Workbook. Choose five events from the TV article in Exercise 1 or the conversation in Exercise 3 above. Write statements using *ago*.

In order to understand time order in a listening test, take notes if the test lets you. In your notes, show how one event follows another. Maybe put years in order. Maybe use arrows or timelines.

### Saying how you feel

Some words and phrases show positive or negative feelings about something. For example, *too soft* and *bad* are negative. *Delicious* and *favorite* are positive. Many tests ask about feelings.

## 1 Understanding positive or negative feelings

AUDIO FILE 🔊 Listen to or read the conversation. Mark each statement as *P* (positive) or *N* (negative).

1. ____ This lettuce looks old.

2. ____ They come from too far away.

3. ____ I want some nice hot peppers with it.

4. ____ There's nothing wrong with red meat.

**Susan** This is a really good buffet, Philip. This pasta looks great. Just like in Italy.

**Philip** Maybe, Susan, but look at this salad bar. This lettuce looks old.

**Susan** Yeah, that's a problem with a lot of fruits and vegetables. They come from too far away.

**Philip** Yeah. They get soft when they're transported.

**Susan** Or some kinds of fruit are too firm. Like these tomatoes. They're almost hard!

**Philip** I know. Farmers grow kinds that can travel without getting soft, but those kinds don't have any taste.

**Susan** Strawberries can be like that, too. Too hard and tasteless.

**Philip** But anyway, your chicken pasta looks great.

**Susan** Yeah. The pasta is OK, but the chicken is kind of boring. I want some nice hot peppers with it.

**Philip** Peppers? With chicken pasta? You must be joking.

**Susan** Hey, I like peppers. With any food.

**Philip** You're crazy. I don't like hot peppers at all. Too spicy.

**Susan** So what are you going to have?

**Philip** You're going to think this is gross, but I'm going to have a burger.

**Susan** Red meat? That's really bad for you.

**Philip** There's nothing wrong with red meat. It's healthy.

**Susan** No, it's not. All that fat is going to give you heart problems later.

**Philip** I'll take that chance. I like it.

**Susan** What about dessert? Want some ice cream?

**Philip** Dessert? Ice cream? Talk about too much fat! That stuff is terrible.

**Susan** Well, you have your favorites, and I have mine.

**Philip** That's true. *Bon appetit!*

## 2 Understanding how people feel about things

AUDIO FILE 🔊 Listen to or read the conversation again. Check (✓) the things Susan and Philip have positive feelings about. Write *X* next to the things they have negative feelings about.

| | Susan | Philip |
|---|---|---|
| 1. the fruit and vegetables | | |
| 2. the chicken pasta | | |
| 3. hot peppers | | |
| 4. red meat | | |

Strategies for taking the: **TOEFL® Test** **TOEIC® Test** **IELTS™ Test**

You classify things by putting them into groups. Recognizing the groups is important in understanding a reading or listening passage. You might have to put things into groups on a test.

## 3 Putting things into groups

Read the article about diets. Circle the word that does NOT belong in each group.

| | | | |
|---|---|---|---|
| 1. Things that give you vitamin C | oranges | potatoes | white bread |
| 2. Things with a lot of carbohydrates | spinach | pasta | rice |
| 3. Things with good fat | olive oil | bacon | fish |
| 4. Things that give you fiber | pears | celery | eggs |

# To Your Health: A Good Diet

A well-known saying is, "You are what you eat." It's important to eat the right foods to give your body the vitamins, fats, and other things it needs.

Vitamin C is extremely important. It helps you fight colds and heal quickly if you have a cut or bruise. It also helps make bones and muscles strong. Everyone knows that fruits like oranges and apples have vitamin C. So do peppers, broccoli, lettuce, and even potatoes.

Your body also needs carbohydrates for energy. Before a long race, many runners eat a lot of pasta, whole-wheat bread, or brown rice to get energy. These carbohydrates can be good, but other foods contain carbohydrates that don't give much useful energy and can make you fat. Cakes and other sweet things, bread made from white flour, and white rice are some of those foods.

Surprisingly, we all need fats, and some fats are good. Fatty meat like bacon and some kinds of oil can be bad for you. They can keep your heart from doing its best. But other fats in foods like fish, olive oil, some nuts, and soybeans are actually good.

Finally, we all need fiber. Celery, spinach, whole wheat, and crispy fruits like pears and apples have a lot of fiber. Foods like cheese or eggs do not. Fiber is like rough little pieces of food. They help your body break apart the other foods you eat. Without enough fiber, your stomach may feel too full or upset.

## 4 Check your understanding

Read the article again. Write *T* for true or *F* for false.

1. ____ Many runners eat cakes before a race to get energy.

2. ____ Potatoes contain vitamin C.

3. ____ Your body will be healthier if you eat no fats.

> There are many ways to identify different groups of details. Sometimes each paragraph is about one group. Also, look at the question. Does it contain the names of any groups? Look for these group names in the reading.

## 5 Skills in review

Look at the shopping list on page 64 of the Student Book. Make another shopping list so you can get all the good things mentioned in the reading in Exercise 3.

# Unit 10 | Inferences and word combinations

## Making inferences about people

Writers and speakers often communicate things without saying them directly. When you guess about the writer's or speaker's meaning, you make an *inference*. Inferences come from many things, including word clues, personal experiences, and logic.

**1 What is an inference?**

Read the e-mail. Make inferences. Circle the best word or phrase.

1. The guy from Kari's math class likes (math / cowboys / rock music).

2. Kari's roommate (cares about / doesn't like / is smarter than) other people.

3. Kari is interested in (sports / jokes / money).

| To: | Ed Mason |
|---|---|
| From: | Kari Cooper |
| Date: | November 5 |
| Subject: | College life |

Hi Ed,

What's up? I have a short break between classes, so I wanted to write. I have a very busy schedule, with a lot of hard classes. I'm meeting a lot of unusual people, too! Every day, this guy in my math class wears a T-shirt with the name of a rock band on it. He must have hundreds of them. A girl in my dorm has long hair that is a different color every day. Today it's bright blue. And one of my professors wears a formal suit and tie ALL THE TIME! Even at a football game last Saturday, everybody else was wearing T-shirts and jeans, but not him.

Not everyone is weird. My roommate is great. She listens to music while studying, but she always uses earphones. And she never uses my stuff without asking. I also have some close friends from my music class. There's Bob, who always makes us laugh. Chrissie wears really expensive clothes, but she's not like you might think. She doesn't spend lots of money on shopping or anything. Then there's Dana, who's a lot like me. She played soccer in high school. Sometimes we go running together.

I hope you can visit some time. I want you to meet my friends. Maybe we can go out to dinner or see a movie or something? Hope to see you soon!

Kari

## Combinations with adjectives and nouns

Some adjectives often go with certain nouns. For example, *cloudy* often goes with *day* or *sky*. Test questions might ask you to match adjectives with nouns or to understand descriptions that use adjectives.

**2 Adjectives that go with nouns**

Read the e-mail again. Complete each sentence with an adjective from the list.

Strategies for taking the:   TOEFL® Test     TOEIC® Test     IELTS™ Test

| expensive | close | formal | long |

1. I have some _____ friends at school.
2. Chrissie wears _____ clothes.
3. She has _____ blue hair.
4. The professor wears _____ clothes, including a suit and tie.

### 3  Choosing the best adjective

AUDIO FILE 🔊 Listen to or read the interview. Match each adjective to a noun. Write the letter of the adjective.

| Nouns | Adjectives |
|---|---|
| 1. ____  advice | a. late |
| 2. ____  career | b. soft |
| 3. ____  night | c. successful |
| 4. ____  voice | d. wise |

| Interviewer | Hello. Today I'm talking with the popular singer Penny Jones. Welcome, Penny. |
|---|---|
| Penny | Thanks. |
| Interviewer | You've had a successful career in music. How did you do it? |
| Penny | Well, first of all, hard work. |
| Interviewer | What do you mean? |
| Penny | Being a musician is more than bright lights and big crowds. |
| Interviewer | So you mean you have to study hard at music school? |
| Penny | Not just that. Practice. That means a lot of late nights. |
| Interviewer | Were your parents musicians? Did you grow up with music? |

| Penny | My family is very close. My dad had some wise advice, "Do it while you're young." |
|---|---|
| Interview | And that means… |
| Penny | Well, if you have a strong desire to do something, don't wait. |
| Interviewer | Did you follow his advice? |
| Penny | I first sang as a little girl. My voice was so soft, no one could hear me. I needed professional help! |
| Interviewer | And you got it? |
| Penny | Yes. I went to the Stone Music School. My teachers were very strict. They helped me grow. |

### 4  Check your understanding

AUDIO FILE 🔊 Listen to or read the interview again. Circle the best answer to each question.

1. What kind of work does Penny do?

   a. singing      b. teaching      c. playing piano

2. Who told Penny to start singing early?

   a. a teacher      b. a musician      c. her father

3. At first, Penny was too ____.

   a. quiet      b. tired      c. strict

> Pay attention to adjectives that appear with nouns in newspapers, magazines, and books. Make a list of these pairs and see how often they appear in your readings. Try using them in conversation and in your writing.

### 5  Skills in review

Look at the pictures in Exercise 5 on page 46 of the Workbook. What inferences can you make about Alice, George, and Manuel?

**Predictions:** *what, when, how likely?*

A *prediction* is a guess about the future. To answer test questions about predictions, you need to understand many things: What is going to happen? When is it going to happen? How likely is it to happen?

## 1 Understanding predictions about the weather

**AUDIO FILE** 🔊 Listen to or read the weather report. Fill in each blank with the best word or phrase.

| cooler | drier | warmer | wetter |
|---|---|---|---|

1. Tonight is probably going to be _____ than tomorrow night.
2. Tomorrow is probably going to be _____ than today.
3. Monday is probably going to be _____ than Tuesday.
4. Tuesday is probably going to be _____ than Monday.

# Weather Report

Good morning. FM 103.9 weather here. We have a great day ahead of us today. It is going to be sunny and warm all day. After yesterday's rain, we all need some sun, and we are going to get it today for sure. Not a cloud in the sky right now here in the city, and it's going to stay that way all day. High temperatures today are going to be in the low 70s—a perfect day to get out there and take a walk, ride your bike, whatever.

Tonight is also going to be clear, but a little bit cool. Temperatures are going to get down into the low 50s. So you need a jacket if you go out tonight. Tomorrow morning is going to be nice and sunny, too, but look for some clouds during the afternoon. There is a very small chance of a little light rain tomorrow afternoon, but I don't think most of us are going to get any. Those clouds are going to make us a little cooler than today. High temperatures tomorrow are going to be only in the upper 60s.

Then tomorrow night the rain moves in. I'm almost 100 percent sure about that rain. Some places in the city could get a lot of rain tomorrow night—maybe an inch. The rain is going to continue into Monday, again almost a 100 percent chance. Looking ahead to Tuesday, we are going to dry out—maybe a little bit of rain in the morning, but not a strong chance. I think Tuesday is going to be mostly sunny. Look for temperatures Monday and Tuesday in the upper 60s. After that, our next chance of rain might come next weekend. But that's far in the future. We can't be sure. Keep listening to our weather forecasts here on FM 103.9 for updates.

## 2 How likely is it?

*Likely* means "almost sure to happen." Listen to or read the weather report again. Check (✓) each thing that is likely to happen.

1. ____ sunny weather today
2. ____ rain tomorrow night
3. ____ sunny weather Monday
4. ____ rain next weekend

Strategies for taking the:   ( TOEFL® Test )   ( TOEIC® Test )   ( IELTS™ Test )

In some predictions, different people are going to do different things. You have to understand who is going to act. A test question may ask you to match a future action with a person.

**3 Identifying who is going to do something**

Read the program for a graduation ceremony. Circle the correct word or phrase.

1. The college president is going to (start / end) the ceremony.

2. The top student is going to (present degrees / give a speech).

3. Parents are going to (have coffee / sing the college song).

# Landon College Graduation

| Time | Event | Presenter |
|------|-------|-----------|
| 9:00 | Welcome to Guests | Prof. Mary Tate, President, Landon College |
| 9:15 | School Song | College Band / All Faculty, Students |
| 9:30 | Goodbye Speech | James Cole, Valedictorian (top student) |
| 9:45 | Guest Speech | Governor Kevin Jones |
| 10:00 | Presentation of Degrees to Graduating Students | Prof. Mary Tate |
| 10:20 | Senior Class Song | College Band / Bob Haley (singer) |
| 10:25 | End of Ceremony | Dr. Len Gordon, Dean, History Department |
| 10:30–11:30 | Coffee and Cake | Parents, Graduates, and College Faculty |

**4 Check your understanding**

Read the program again. Write an answer on each line.

1. Who is going to play two songs?

   _____

2. How many speeches are going to be given by a student?

   _____

3. Which event is going to include a speech by a dean?

   _____

**5 Skills in review**

Look at Exercise 2 on page 50 of the Workbook. Make sentences using *going to* about the Landon College graduation ceremony in Exercise 3 above. Mention these people: Mary Tate, James Cole, Len Gordon, and Kevin Jones.

Listen or read to find words or phrases like *sure* (very likely), *probably* (likely), *possibly* (a little bit likely), and *probably not* (unlikely). They can tell you how likely something is to happen.

# Unit 12 | Present perfect and time phrases

## Present perfect verbs for actions that still continue

A *present perfect* verb often shows that an action started in the past and still continues. A *simple past* verb is for an action only in the past. Test questions often ask about this difference.

### 1 Noticing present perfect verbs

Read the letter. Check (✓) each action that continues into the present.

1. ____ Linda often thinks of Jenny.

2. ____ Jenny jumps in a hole.

3. ____ Jimmy Barrett wins tennis tournaments.

February 10

Dear Jenny,

I haven't heard from you since Christmas. How have you been? Are you too busy to write to your old friend? Just kidding! I know you're busy.

I just looked at some old pictures of us—I mean really old! Remember when we went on that class trip to the beach in elementary school? That's right. Ten years ago. That's amazing. They're really cool pictures. In one, you and I are digging a big hole in the sand. I think I remember that. You jumped in the hole, I think, and I started filling it with sand. You got really scared!

You and I have been friends for a long time—more than ten years. Life has taken us in different directions, but we're still friends, right? Even though you never write letters to me! Again, just kidding. Oh, before I forget: Do you remember little Jimmy Barrett? The kid with red hair who moved to Florida? Well, he's a great tennis player now. I saw him on TV last weekend, playing in a big tournament. The announcer said he has won ten big tournaments since he started college. Amazing.

Anyway, that's all for now. I hope college is going OK. Write when you get a chance!

Love,

Linda

## Time phrases with *for* and *since*

Phrases with *for* and *since* go with present perfect verbs. *For* indicates a period of time. *Since* indicates a point in the past. Test questions may ask you to understand the difference or to use *for/since* correctly.

### 2 Using *for* and *since*

Read the letter again. Write *for* or *since*.

1. Jenny and Linda have been friends _____ more than 10 years.

2. Linda hasn't heard from Jenny _____ Christmas.

3. Jimmy Barrett has been winning tennis tournaments _____ he started college.

Strategies for taking the:    ( TOEFL® Test )    ( TOEIC® Test )    ( IELTS™ Test )

## 3 Practicing with *for* / *since*

AUDIO FILE 🔊 Listen to or read the conversation. Circle the correct words or phrases.

1. Stella and Ron (have started / started) working at noon. They have worked (for / since) two hours.

2. Ron (has gone / went) to the store two days ago. He has had some marker pens (for / since) then.

3. Stella has tried e-mailing Dr. Moore (for / since) Monday. She (hasn't heard / didn't hear) from him for three days.

4. Stella and Ron (have answered / answered) four questions (for / since) last week.

| | | | |
|---|---|---|---|
| **Stella** | Ron, we have been working on this for two hours! | **Stella** | And we did one yesterday. And… |
| **Ron** | Really? Let's see, we started… | **Ron** | One today—so far. No, sorry. We've done four, not five. |
| **Stella** | At noon. We've been working since 12 o'clock. I need a break. | **Stella** | I'm still not sure how many questions we have to do. |
| **Ron** | OK, but first let's check what we've done. | **Ron** | Ten, I think. But maybe not. Maybe nine. |
| **Stella** | Well, we've bought all the paper we need. | **Stella** | We have to ask. I've been trying to reach Dr. Moore for three days. Since Monday. |
| **Ron** | And marker pens. I got them Tuesday at the bookstore. Two days ago. | **Ron** | No answer? |
| **Stella** | OK. So, how many questions have we answered? | **Stella** | No answer. Maybe he's out of town and can't get e-mail. |
| **Ron** | Five, right? We did two when we started last week. | **Ron** | Let's just keep working on the questions. I'm sure we'll reach him soon. |

## 4 Check your understanding

AUDIO FILE 🔊 Listen to or read the conversation again. Write *T* for true or *F* for false.

1. _____ Ron and Stella are working together now.

2. _____ Ron has done five questions, but Stella has done only four.

3. _____ Ron and Stella are not sure how many questions they have to do.

## 5 Skills in review

Look at the chart in Exercise 1 on page 56 of the Workbook. Choose five verbs from the personal letter to Jenny in Exercise 1 above and make a similar chart using past simple and past participle.

> Questions like *What have you done?* ask about experiences from the past to now. They use a present perfect verb, but answers can include both present perfect verbs (for things still happening) and simple past verbs (for things that have already ended).

# Answer Key

## Unit 1 (pp. 2–3)

1 **Listening for personal information**  Check 1

2 **Personal information on a form**  First name: Jenny; Hometown: Springport, Ohio; Dorm on campus: Anders Hall

3 **Working with information on a form**  1. a; 2. c; 3. a

4 **Check your understanding**  Check 2, 3, 4

5 **Skills in review**  Answers will vary.

## Unit 2 (pp. 4–5)

1 **Using pronouns**  1. campus; 2. classes; 3. Monica and Zara; 4. Zara's father; 5. Monica's parents

2 **Understanding possessive nouns**  1. university's; 2. professor's; 3. Malaysia's

3 **Practice with possessive nouns**  1. Dan; 2. Tina's father; 3. Mary; 4. Steve

4 **Check your understanding**  1. F; 2. F; 3. T; 4. T

5 **Skills in review**  Answers will vary.

## Unit 3 (pp. 6–7)

1 **Understanding what people usually do**  Check 1, 3, 5, 6

2 **Understanding who does an action**  1. J; 2. K; 3. J; 4. K

3 **Who does each job?**  1. pilot; 2. Web Manager; 3. gate agent; 4. flight attendant

4 **Check your understanding**  1. Web Manager; 2. Flight attendants; 3. Flight attendants; 4. co-pilot

5 **Skills in review**  Answers will vary.

## Unit 4 (pp. 8–9)

1 **Understanding positive and negative verbs**  1. has; 2. cannot; 3. bought; 4. drives

2 **My favorite things**  1. cats; 2. Kari; 3. piano

3 **Listening for favorites**  Tom's favorites: sports, biking; movies, action; food to cook, Italian. Dana's favorites: sports, skiing; movies, mysteries; food to cook, Indian

4 **Check your understanding**  1. T; 2. F; 3. T

5 **Skills in review**  Answers will vary.

## Unit 5 (pp. 10–11)

1 **Welcome to Camptown College**  1. There is; 2. there are; 3. There are; 4. there is

2 **Understanding descriptions of places**  1. b; 2. c; 3. a

3 **Prepositions showing where something is**  1. in; 2. under; 3. through

4 **Check your understanding**  1. in; 2. in front of or below; 3. behind

5 **Skills in review**  Answers will vary.

## Unit 6 (pp. 12–13)

1 **Talking about abilities**  Check 1

2 **Timed speaking practice**  Answers will vary.

3 **Practicing forms of *can***  1. can; 2. could; 3. couldn't; 4. can't

4 **Check your understanding**  1. b; 2. b; 3. a

5 **Skills in review**  Answers will vary.

## Unit 7 (pp. 14–15)

1 **Using time expressions** Correct order: 3, 1, 2, 4

2 **Check your understanding** 1. a; 2. a; 3. a

3 **Understanding how speakers say dates** 1. a; 2. b; 3. b

4 **Check your understanding** 1. T; 2. T; 3. T

5 **Skills in review** Answers will vary.

## Unit 8 (pp. 16–17)

1 **Using expressions to understand time** Order: 2, 4, 3, 1

2 **How to say the names of years** Answers will vary.

3 **Understanding years in speech** 1. 1990; 2. 1979; 3. 1993; 4. 1985

4 **Check your understanding** 1. T; 2. F; 3. T; 4. T

5 **Skills in review** Answers will vary.

## Unit 9 (pp. 18–19)

1 **Understanding positive or negative feelings** 1. N; 2. N; 3. P; 4. P

2 **Understanding how people feel about things** 1. Susan X and Philip X; 2. Susan X and Philip ✓; 3. Susan ✓ and Philip X; 4. Susan X and Philip ✓

3 **Putting things into groups** 1. white bread; 2. spinach; 3. bacon; 4. eggs

4 **Check your understanding** 1. F; 2. T; 3. F

5 **Skills in review** Answers will vary.

## Unit 10 (pp. 20–21)

1 **What is an inference?** 1. rock music; 2. cares about; 3. sports

2 **Adjectives that go with nouns** 1. close; 2. expensive; 3. long; 4. formal

3 **Choosing the best adjective** 1. d; 2. c; 3. a; 4. b

4 **Check your understanding** 1. a; 2. c; 3. a

5 **Skills in review** Answers will vary.

## Unit 11 (pp. 22–23)

1 **Understanding predictions about the weather** 1. drier; 2. cooler; 3. wetter; 4. warmer

2 **How likely is it?** Check 1 and 2

3 **Identifying who is going to do something** 1. start; 2. give a speech; 3. have coffee

4 **Check your understanding** 1. the college band; 2. one; 3. the end of the ceremony

5 **Skills in review** Answers will vary.

## Unit 12 (pp. 24–25)

1 **Noticing present perfect verbs** Check 1 and 3

2 **Using *for* and *since*** 1. for; 2. since; 3. since

3 **Practicing with *for* / *since*** 1. started / for; 2. went / since; 3. since / hasn't heard; 4. have answered / since

4 **Check your understanding** 1. T; 2. F; 3. T

5 **Skills in review** Answers will vary.

**OXFORD**
UNIVERSITY PRESS

198 Madison Avenue
New York, NY 10016 USA
Great Clarendon Street, Oxford OX2 6DP UK

Oxford University Press is a department of the University of Oxford.
It furthers the University's objective of excellence in research, scholarship,
and education by publishing worldwide in

Oxford   New York

Auckland   Cape Town   Dar es Salaam   Hong Kong   Karachi
Kuala Lumpur   Madrid   Melbourne   Mexico City   Nairobi
New Delhi   Shanghai   Taipei   Toronto

With offices in

Argentina   Austria   Brazil   Chile   Czech Republic   France   Greece
Guatemala   Hungary   Italy   Japan   Poland   Portugal   Singapore
South Korea   Switzerland   Thailand   Turkey   Ukraine   Vietnam

OXFORD and OXFORD ENGLISH are registered trademarks of Oxford University
Press in certain countries.

© Oxford University Press 2009

Database right Oxford University Press (maker)

Editorial Director: Laura Pearson
Publishing Manager: Erik Gundersen
Managing Editor: Louisa van Houten
Development Editor: Rosi Perea
Design Director: Susan Sanguily
Design Manager: Maj-Britt Hagsted
Senior Designer: Michael Steinhofer
Image Editor: Robin Fadool
Design Production Manager: Stephen White
Production Editors: Alissa Heyman, Greg Johnson
Manufacturing Manager: Shanta Persaud
Manufacturing Coordinator: Elizabeth Matsumoto

ISBN: 978-0-19-472951-2

Printed in China

10   9   8   7   6

This book is printed on paper from certified and well-managed sources.

**ACKNOWLEDGMENTS**

*Illustrations by*: Joanna Kerr pp. 5, 6, 23, 48; Ned Jolliffe pp. 9, 10, 13, 25, 52; Mark
Duffin pp. 16, 58; Ana Diaz pp. 21, 27; Dettmer Otto p. 33; John Holder pp. 38,
39; Ian Kellas p. 57.

*Commissioned Photography by*: Gareth Boden pp. 2, 4, 6, 26, 31, 41, 51, 59; Maggie
Milner pp. 9, 51, 55.

*The publishers would like to thank the following for their kind permission to reproduce
photographs*: Superstock: Angelo Cavalli p. 2 (Mexico City); JLImages/Alamy: p. 2
(Boston); Danita Delimont: p. 2 (Seoul); istockphoto: p. 2 (Rome); Panorama
Images The Image Works: p. 2 (Beijing); Pictures Colour Library p. 2 (Mount
Fuji, Sydney, p. 2 (Ayers Rock/Charles Bowman), Punchstock p. 2 (smiling man/
Photodisc, friends/Image Source), Lonely Planet Images p. 2; Getty Images p. 2
(woman in white blouse, couple/Stone), Getty Images p. 2 (two girls/The Image
Bank, businessman/ Taxi); Punchstock p. 3 (portrait of a woman/Photodisc),
Getty Images p. 3 (young man/The Image Bank), Getty Images p. 3 (couple/
Stone), OUP p. 4 (Flags/Clip Art), Shutterstock: pp. 5, 6 (eagle stamp); Pictures

Colour Library p. 7 (Moscow/Charles Bowman), Punchstock p. 7 (portrait of
a woman/Photodisc, businessman/Bananastock), Corbis p. 7 (two girls/Roger
Ressmeyer), OUP p. 8 (dark haired woman/Corbis), Punchstock p. 9 (mature
woman/BlueMoon Stock, man in woods/Thinkstock), Education Photos p. 9
(schoolgirl/John Walmsley); Getty Images p. 9 (teen boy, mature woman/Stone),
Alamy p. 9 (elderly man/Photofusion Picture Library, Ireland/Peter Adams
Photography), Photos.com/Jupiter Unlimited: p. 11; The Image Works: Jeff
Greengerg p. 12 (sales clerk); p. 12 businesswoman wearing headset/image100,
nurse and child/Photodisc, OUP p. 12 (businessman/Photodisc), Punchstock
p. 14 (fashion shoot/Digital Vision), Blend Images/Alamy: Jeremy Woodhouse
p. 14 (bottom); Getty Images p. 15 (tour guide/Stone), Punchstock p. 15 (pilot/
Photodisc), Punchstock p. 17 (couple in airport/Digital Vision), Punchstock p. 18
(travel agent/ Image Source), Getty Images p. 19 (businessman/Taxi), Lonely
Planet Images p. 19 (Black Forest/Esbin Anderson Photography OUP p. 20
(cinema), Punchstock p. 20 (business meeting/Brand X Pictures), Alamy p. 20
(teenagers/images-of-france), Image State/AGE StockFoto: Martyn Goddard p. 22;
Getty Images p. 26 (young man/The Image Bank), Alamy p. 26 (teenage girl/
Goodshoot), Alamy p. 27 (couple/Vladimir Godnik), Punchstock p. 28 (toddler/
Bananastock), Punchstock p. 29 (man on phone/Image Source, woman on
phone, girl on phone/Creatas), Alamy p. 29 (man on phone/Ingram Publishing,
man/plainpicture, girl at computer/ Peter Arnold Inc.), Alamy p. 30 (Switzerland/
Peter Adams Photography), Popperfoto/Getty Images: Paul Popper p. 32; Alamy
p. 35 (vintage telephone/Index Stock), Corbis p. 35 (Alexander Graham Bell/
Bettmann), Corbis p. 37 (man painting/Jose Luis Pelaez), OUP p. 43 (couple
dining/Photodisc), p. 46 (elderly lady with laptop/Tom Stewart, playing soccer/
Johnny Buzzerio), OUP p. 46 (man cooking/Photodisc), p. 47 teenage girl/
Profimedia. CZ s.r.o); Punchstock p. 47 (man jogging/IT Stock Free, p. 47 woman
reading/Creatas), Corbis Punchstock p. 49 (couple shopping/ Image Source,
shopping/Imagestate), Alamy: Russell Kord p. 51 (Montreal); Pictures Colour
Library p. 51 (Rodinara Beach/John Miller), Alamy: Ramona Settle p. 55 (hotel in
Puerto Rico); Getty Images p. 57 (young woman/James Darell/Stone OUP p. 59
(airplane/Photodisc), Punchstock p. 61 (office worker/Big Cheese Photo); OUP
p. 63 (friends, couple/Photodisc); istockphoto: p. 64; OUP p. 66 (smiling man/
photodisc), OUP p. 66 (Rocky Mountain/Corel), OUP p. 67 (chef/Photodisc).

*Commissioned Photography by*: Ken Karp Photography: pp. 2, 26, 59.

*Cover photos*: Pixtal/AGE Fotostock: (top left); Photo Alto/Jupiter Images: James
Hardy (top center); dbimages/Alamy: Roy Johnson (top right); PhotoAlto/AGE
Fotostock/: incent Hazat (left center); Masterfile: (right center); Masterfile:
(bottom right); ASP/Getty Images: Kirstin Scholtz (bottom left).

*The authors and publisher are grateful to those who have given permission to reproduce
the following extracts and adaptations of copyright material*: pp. 38–39 Extracts from
*Oxford Bookworms 2: Stories from Five Towns* by Arnold Bennett. Simplified edition
© Oxford University Press 2000.

*Spotlight on Testing*: pp. 3, 11, 19 (Hispanic female/Fancy/Veer AGE Fotostock);
pp. 5, 13, 21 (Hispanic male/ StockByte/AGE Fotostock/George Doyle); pp. 7,
15, 23 (Asian female/ Tetra Images/ArtLifeImages/Superstock); pp. 9, 17, 25
(Caucasian male/ Westend61/ArtLifeImages/Superstock/Hanno Keppel).